Faith in Trials

By

Nicole Vo

Nicole Vo

ISBN-13

Dedication

To my daughter Kylie,

I never imagined I would raise you as a single mother. That was not the life I had planned for you. But life unfolds in ways we don't expect, and this journey gave me strength I never knew I carried inside me.

Our special bond began when you were just four months old. I remember holding you in my arms, filled with fear of so many unknowns. In that moment, I made a promise to myself — that I would never fail you as your mother.

You had a difficult upbringing. There were many nights when I struggled to balance the demands of my career while trying to be the mother you deserved. I fought desperately to create stability for us. I uprooted you more times than I can count, yet through it all, you transitioned with such grace. Being your mother has been one of the greatest honors of my life.

I learned to be strong and resilient so I could give you the healthiest and happiest childhood possible. When our financial situation improved, I was finally able to buy our first home — a place where you had a bedroom of your own. We started our annual "mommy and me" vacations, creating memories that will forever live in my heart.

Even through the most challenging times, I always tried to be the best mother I could be. I know you watched me — the way I carried myself, the way I handled stress, and the many trials life placed in front of us. I know your heart broke when I went through criminal prosecution and suffered my traumatic brain injury. But I also know you saw my bravery. You saw my courage.

We shared years of tears together, not knowing what the future held. What kept me together was my unwavering faith in the Lord. I hope when you read this, it inspires you to believe in yourself no matter how difficult life becomes.

Nicole Vo

Always remember: your circumstances do not define you. When your mind is clear and your faith is strong, you can overcome anything that comes your way.

Thank you for being my daily reminder that failure is not an option. Our bond is deep, unbreakable, and incredibly special. I am forever honored to be your mom.

This book, and every victory behind it, is for you.

Acknowledgments

First and foremost, I give all glory and honor to God. His grace carried me through seasons I did not think I would survive, and His faithfulness made this book possible.

To my dearest husband Tim—

Thank you for being my steady place in every storm and my strength when mine was running low. Your support, patience, and quiet confidence carried me through some of the hardest seasons of my life.

You never tried to take the weight from me — you simply stood beside me while I carried it, reminding me I was never alone. Your belief in me never wavered, even when I doubted myself.

When I was faced with criminal prosecution, you refused to give up-pouring every ounce of your heart, strength, and investigative skills into fighting for my innocence.

When I recovered from brain surgery, you nurtured me back to wellness helping me overcome the challenges that followed.

This journey, every lesson, and every victory holds your fingerprints. I am stronger because you walk with me, and braver because you stand behind me.

With all my love and gratitude -Nicole

To my brother Mike —

My big brother. Aside from our dad, you are the strongest man I know.

It brings me great joy that together we were able to fulfill our parents' dream for us. Having you stand beside me as one of my attorneys during my criminal prosecution was nothing short of a blessing from the Lord. You gave everything — your time, your finances, time away from your own family, and your legal expertise

— to take on the toughest case of your life: fighting for your little sister's freedom.

You knew I was innocent from the very beginning. You never doubted. You stood firm in your belief that the truth would prevail, even when the road was long and emotionally exhausting. The trauma weighed heavily on our entire family, but you held us together like glue.

I am deeply grateful for your commitment to justice, your sacrifice, and your determination to protect not only me, but the integrity of our family name.

With love and endless gratitude- your sister.

To my mother - Charlie

You are the strongest woman I know and one of my greatest role models in life.

Growing up, I watched you build a life through sheer determination and sacrifice. With little English but limitless drive, you carved your own path through career and entrepreneurship. You worked tirelessly, often carrying burdens no one else could see, so your children could have opportunities you never had. You showed me what perseverance truly looks like — not through words, but through the way you lived each day.

You led us by example: honor the family name, move with integrity, and never stop pursuing the American dream. Through your sacrifices, you gave us stability, discipline, and values that continue to guide me. From you, I learned the importance of respect for family, humility, faith, and quiet strength — traditions deeply rooted in our culture that I now carry forward with pride.

You held yourself with grace and dignity, earning deep respect within the Vietnamese community and beyond. Even when life was difficult, you remained composed, resilient, and unwavering in your love for your children.

Even from a distance, I was always watching and learning. The strength and resilience people see in me began with you. Those qualities are part of your legacy, and I carry them with honor.

Thank you for your sacrifices, your love, and the foundation you gave me to stand on.

With love and deep gratitude - Ni.

To my friend and criminal defense attorney- HS

You were not placed in my life by coincidence — you were sent by God at the exact moment I needed you most. From the day criminal charges were filed, I knew in my spirit that the Lord had chosen you to stand with me.

I will never find words big enough for what you did. Through long, weary nights, you poured over every page of discovery with relentless focus, leaving no detail untouched. Your endurance, discipline, and commitment never wavered. Every time we spoke, I felt peace, knowing you were fighting with the strength, conviction, and purpose of someone carrying a calling — not just a case.

When I was overwhelmed, you stood firm. When fear tried to rise, your confidence steadied me. You carried a cross that was not yours to bear, yet you bore it with grace, courage, and faith. You believed in my innocence without hesitation, and you trusted that God's truth would prevail.

Because of your obedience to that calling and your relentless pursuit of justice, the truth came to light and my freedom was restored. I will forever see your presence in that season as one of God's greatest mercies in my life.

I carry lifelong gratitude in my heart for you.

To my best friend, Erica —

Nicole Vo

Our friendship spans more than three decades, and the memories we share are treasures I hold close to my heart.

You have stood beside me through every chapter of my life — from Kylie's birth, to the end of two marriages, through the gut-wrenching pain of my criminal prosecution, and the long road of healing after major brain surgery. In my darkest moments and my strongest ones, you never left my side.

Thank you for standing beside me through every trial, setback, and victory. Your encouragement, patience, and understanding carried me through moments when I did not have the strength on my own.

Your heart is one of the biggest I know. Your loyalty, compassion, and unconditional love carried me more than you will ever fully understand.

My heart is full because you walked through life with me. I am deeply grateful for you and truly blessed to call you my best friend.

To my dear family and friends-

To the Vo and Nguyen side of the family –When everything had been stripped away from me, you carried me through with emotional and financial support. Your unconditional love sustained me through the darkest seasons of my life, and I am forever grateful.

The Lam family – My loving extended family. Thank you for being such a constant source of strength in my life and for being the most amazing Aunties to Kylie. I'm beyond grateful that you've given her the kind of normal, loving childhood every child deserves.

My colleagues at the DA's office – Thank you for believing in me when everything around us felt surreal.

My friends at the Public Defender's Office and Private Defense Bar. You believed in me when wrongful criminal charges were announced. You were ready, willing, and able to assist in my defense. You listened without judgment, prayed when I couldn't find the words, and reminded me who I was when life tried to make me forget. Your refusal to let me give up, even when the road felt impossible, meant more than I can ever express.

For that, I am eternally grateful.

To the Judges I've appeared in front of – You stood by me with your unconditional support believing that in the end, justice would prevail.

To all the Law Enforcement Officers I have worked with. You stood by me when the system turned against me. Thank you for walking alongside me.

To Elizabeth - Every call, message, prayer, and act of kindness helped lift me through one of the most difficult seasons of my life. Healing after brain surgery is a difficult journey. In moments when I broke down, you listened with compassion, and when my mind was at its weakest, you stepped in with clarity. You are the impetus for writing this book. You put my thoughts into action. You reminded me that my story is unique and purposeful, not one to be wasted but shared for a reason greater than myself. With heartfelt gratitude, thank you for being a part of my story.

Table of Contents

Dedication.................... iii

Acknowledgments v

Preface 1

Chapter One: Born of Escape 3

Chapter Two: Becoming American 6

Chapter Three: The Anchor & The Cage 10

Chapter Four: It begins at USC 13

Chapter Five: Early Law School 18

Chapter Six: A Mother 25

Chapter Seven: Swearing In Ceremony 29

Chapter Eight: The Badge Ceremony.................... 33

Chapter Nine: Voices in the Courtroom 37

Chapter Ten: A Marriage That Should Have Never Been 41

Chapter Eleven: The Wrath That Came 49

Chapter Twelve: My God, My Living Hope 57

Chapter Thirteen: Rebuilding 67

Chapter Fourteen: A Friend in Him.................... 71

Chapter Fifteen: God Is Still Writing My Story 79

Chapter Sixteen: Embracing the New Nicole.................... 82

Chapter Seventeen: What God Has Taught My Heart 84

Final Thoughts From the Author 86

Preface

Even before I knew God, He was writing my story. His hand was there in my parents' bravery, in every miracle that carried us through. And later, when storms came into my own life—storms I could not have imagined—He reminded me that He has given me a spirit of faith and not fear.

My story began long before I could form a memory. I was too young to recall the midnight escapes, the prison walls that held my father, or the weeks at sea on a tiny wooden boat. But my parents' voices have painted those scenes for me all my life.

They were running from a country that no longer felt like home. When Saigon fell and the communists seized power, freedom was stripped from people like my father—educated men viewed as enemies of the new regime. He had taken law and accounting classes before the war, and that alone marked him as a threat. On their first attempt to flee, my parents were caught; my father was sent to a prison camp for a year.

My mother carried my brother and I alone, fearing she might never see him again, fearing what life as a widow under the regime would look like. Trauma made them quiet about those years, but even in their silence, I could feel the weight of what they endured.

My family escaped under a moonless sky, boarding a wooden boat with other desperate families. The communists patrolled the shores. Getting caught again could mean prison, or worse. Instead, they pushed off into open water, leaving everything they knew behind. For weeks, they drifted across an endless ocean, unsure if they would live to see another dawn. Some boats never made it. Ours reached Hong Kong, where we spent time in a refugee camp before a letter—a single letter from a stranger who sponsored our family—changed the entire trajectory of our lives. That letter carried us to America, to the land where my parents could finally plant roots.

Nicole Vo

We arrived with nothing but faith and determination. My parents didn't speak English, didn't have a safety net, but they worked with relentless grit. My mother, with her creative hands, learned cosmetology, rented a small booth in a nail salon, and eventually built a franchise of ten thriving salons before moving into manufacturing. My father worked long hours bookkeeping. Together, they became pioneers in their community; humble people who created a legacy not through wealth, but through sacrifice and faith.

I chose to write this book now because I believe stories can heal—not just the storyteller, but the ones who hear it. For years, I carried pieces of my journey quietly. The trauma my family experienced when they fled, the pain I endured as an adult, the moments when fear nearly crushed me. But through it all, God was weaving a greater purpose. If you have ever wondered whether you could survive what feels impossible, whether broken beginnings can lead to beautiful endings, I want my life to be proof that they can.

I don't share this story because it is perfect. I share it because it is real. Because I have lived through the nights of terror and the mornings of grace. My family's escape was only the beginning. What followed was a life of highs and lows, triumphs and heartbreaks: standing in courtrooms fighting for children, surviving abuse, facing wrongful charges, and even battling for my health after brain surgery. Through it all, one truth remained unshaken: God's goodness outlasts every storm.

If you take anything from these pages, let it be this: miracles still happen. Broken lives can be restored. *Fear doesn't get the final word.* And if my story can help even one person keep pressing forward, then everything I endured has meaning.

My life began as a child in need of protection. God's greatest gift was allowing me to become the protector. His story is my story. My story is His to tell.

Yours truly,

Nicole Vo—

Chapter One: Born of Escape

Trauma has a way of silencing even the strongest warriors. I wish I could tell you every detail of my parents' escape. The nights of fear, the prayers whispered into the dark, but they rarely spoke about those years. Maybe the memories hurt too much. Maybe some stories are too heavy for words.

Still, I can imagine it.

The night sky stretched endlessly above them, black as ink, dotted with stars that offered no comfort. The sea was a restless beast of course, its waves slapping against the fragile wooden boat, almost as if testing how long it would hold. I picture the sting of saltwater on their lips, the sharp bite of wind, and the sound of a baby crying somewhere in the shadows. Every creak of the boat must have felt like a warning. Every splash like a threat.

Before that night, there must have been a stillness. A moment where hope and fear stood side by side. I imagine my mother clutching me close, her heart pounding against my cheek, her mind filled with questions no one could answer:

Would we make it to shore? Would we see the sunrise? Would this child in my arms live to grow up?

Every parent has fears for their children. Hers were life or death.

My father had already endured the unthinkable. Arrested and imprisoned for siding with the South during the Vietnam War, he spent years behind bars not knowing if he would ever hold his family again. When he was finally released, the world he returned to was unrecognizable—home was no longer safe. So, they ran. We ran.

The first escape failed — and the cruel irony is that it was my own cry that betrayed us. Under the cover of a midnight sky, as the boat pushed through dark waters, my infant wail carried louder than the waves. I was barely a year old, too young to understand survival, yet old enough to draw the attention of soldiers. Because of me, my family's desperate bid for freedom was cut short. We were dragged back, defeated and exposed. But giving up was never an option.

When the second attempt was planned, my mother begged to leave me behind in Vietnam with my grandparents. She could not risk another failure. But my grandmother, the immovable matriarch, would not bend. With a voice sharp as steel, she declared,

"No. You go as a family, and you die as a family."

There was no room for negotiation. With a fragile boat, too many bodies crammed together, and the open sea stretching like a dare, we sailed. There were no guarantees, only the choice between staying and dying or leaving and *maybe* living.

I can't tell you what they talked about on that boat because they never told me. But I know trauma leaves fingerprints. I saw it years later in small, ordinary moments—seeing the police in uniform made my mother's hands tremble, how my father's voice grew quiet when the subject of the war came up. Maybe the body remembers what the mouth cannot say.

When we finally reached America, freedom didn't feel like fireworks or parades. It felt like an empty apartment with peeling paint, bare floors, and second-hand furniture. It smelled of dust and uncertainty. Outside, neighbors spoke a language my parents didn't understand. Inside, they had thirty days—thirty days from the generosity of a sponsor family—to figure out a life from scratch.

But even then, my parents knew what mattered most: survival, faith, and a future for their children. My father worked any job he could find, his voice hoarse from practicing English long after the rest of the world slept. My mother enrolled in cosmetology school, one of the few doors open to her without English fluency. It started small, a rented chair in the corner of a nail salon. She bent over strangers' hands with the precision of an artist, painting more than nails.

Faith in Trials

She was painting hope; my beautiful, strong mother.

I remember her coming home late, smelling of acetone and the liquid used as an adhesive for acrylic nails. Her fingers bore the polish stains of other women's beauty, but her face glowed with quiet pride. Word spread quickly: Charlie, the woman with the delicate touch and timeless grace. One client turned into ten, ten into a hundred. Soon, one salon became ten.

Mantrap Nails wasn't just a business. It was a legacy. A story of a woman who turned fear into resilience and calloused hands into opportunity.

Our walls might have been bare, but they were anchored in three values: faith, sacrifice, and education. My parents didn't preach those words; I saw them living it. Every dollar they earned, every hour they worked, was a brick laid in the foundation of our future.

Looking back now, I see God's fingerprints all over those years. Before I ever knew Him, He was already writing my story through their courage. Before I ever stood in a courtroom, He was teaching me what it meant to fight for something bigger than myself. We didn't have much, but we had everything that mattered. And that is where my story begins.

What I didn't know was that everything my parents fought for would one day become the fire in my own fight for justice.

Chapter Two: Becoming American

As a child, of course, I didn't see it that way. To me, becoming American looked like a cheeseburger. The first time I bit into a cheeseburger, I thought I had discovered heaven.

Most American children grew up with McDonald's Happy Meals and drive-thru dinners, but I had never seen anything like it. To me, that yellow paper wrapper might as well have been gold. I stared at what I was holding — two pieces of bread with something tucked inside. A fried patty, a slice of cheese, streaks of ketchup and mustard. It looked messy, almost wrong, but I took a bite anyway. The juices soaked into the bun, the tang of mustard hit the back of my tongue, and I couldn't stop. By the end, I was licking ketchup from my fingers, wide-eyed with wonder.

"Do you like it?" my brother asked, his own mouth already stuffed.

I nodded, grinning. "It's… amazing."

That was my first taste of America.

French fries followed — thin, golden sticks that cracked when I bit them, the salt stinging my lips in the best way. I ate until my belly ached and still wanted more. Every food we tried in those early days felt like stepping into another world. Everything tasted new. Chicken nuggets; tiny squares of meat dipped into sauces I'd never imagined. Fried chicken; crispy skin and mashed potatoes covered in brown gravy. Pizza; gooey cheese that stretched when I pulled my slice away, salty rounds of pepperoni that left grease on my fingers.

Even TV dinners felt like magic: a complete meal divided neatly into trays, ready in five minutes. Salisbury steak, mashed potatoes, corn, and dessert all in one box. I pressed my nose to the glass, watching it spin, convinced America had invented sorcery. Five minutes in a microwave, and dinner was ready. Still, no matter what American foods we discovered, rice never left the center of our table.

I remember the relief on my mother's face the first time she spotted soy sauce in the grocery store. She lifted the bottle with both hands, as if it were a relic she thought lost forever. For a moment, it wasn't just a condiment; it was Vietnam in glass form, a memory she had buried under years of survival suddenly rising to the surface. I remember her lips parting in the faintest smile. In that aisle, surrounded by bright boxes of cereal she couldn't pronounce and canned soups that tasted of salt and nothing else, she had found a piece of home.

Looking back, I think it was more than flavor she was holding on to. It was a reminder that we still belonged somewhere. That even in this new world, with its unfamiliar language and strange customs, pieces of us—our tastes, our roots, our culture—could be carried forward.

Later that night, she poured the dark liquid over steaming rice, and I watched the lines of worry in her face soften just a little.

"We can eat properly now," she whispered.

Finding soy sauce was only the beginning. From time to time, she tried to recreate pho, coaxing broth from ginger and star anise. Without cinnamon sticks or cloves, the taste was always incomplete. She would sip it, sigh, then ladle it into bowls with a shrug.

"Close enough," she said.

Between soy sauce and Salisbury steak, pho and pizza, we learned to live with the in-between. Each meal was a balancing act. One foot planted in the country we had left behind, the other stretching toward the country we were trying to claim. Slowly, clumsily, we were becoming American.

School, however, reminded me that becoming American came at a price.

Nicole Vo

My brother and I were the only Asian children in our classes. Shorter than the others. Yellow skin. Black hair. Brown eyes. The sting of whispers and giggles followed us down the hallways.

"Ching Chong."

"Go back to your country."

It wasn't just words. It was the way kids turned their faces, the way laughter spread like wildfire, leaving me small and burning at the center. The name my mother gave me — *Lai* — became another target. Phonetically, it sounded like "Lie." To a child desperate to blend in, it was unbearable. I tried to fix it by telling classmates the school had made a mistake, that my name was *Lee*. For a short time, even my teacher believed me. But at the next parent-teacher conference, confusion unraveled the lie. My mother corrected him, her voice firm and proud:

"Her name is Lai." And just like that, I was "Lie" again; the girl who could not escape her own name.

"Lie don't lie," they'd chant with smirks, until tears stung my eyes. I began to dread the sound of my own name, the very gift my parents had chosen with love. Unfortunately, our clothes only made things worse. Hand-me-downs worn thin from passing through too many families before us. Shirts with missing buttons. Pants too short, exposing my ankles.

"Flood waters!" the kids laughed, pointing as if they'd discovered something hilarious.

Once, I wore pants with a hole in the crotch. Too embarrassed to tell my mother, I patched them with tape. It didn't hold. After that, I wore dresses year-round, even in the freezing winter. My skin chapped and my legs ached, but at least no one laughed.

The teasing was cruel enough, but sometimes the silence cut deeper. I remember one birthday party in second grade. Every girl in my class received an invitation tucked neatly into their backpacks. Every girl except me. On Monday, they huddled at recess, chattering about the games and the cake, trading candy from their party bags. I stood nearby, pretending to tie my shoelaces, wishing someone would look up and see me.

No one did. I was *invisible*.

When I begged my parents to make the teasing stop, they only said, "Ignore it." To them, words were nothing compared to the dangers they had escaped. But they didn't understand how cruel children could be. They didn't know how every laugh carved itself into me, how silence at the lunch table felt heavier than hunger. And, I was just a child. I wanted to play tag and eat cake and wear pretty clothes like everyone else. Instead, I stayed quiet. Every morning, I swallowed anger and shame with my breakfast rice; dreading that I had to show up at the school again. Every afternoon, I walked home rehearsing in my head what I *should* have said, what I *wished* I could have done. But I never spoke. I just kept walking. And I kept disappearing.

Chapter Three: The Anchor & The Cage

"And we know that God works everything for good, for those who love him and were called according to his purpose." – Romans 8:28 (JVK)

I keep this chapter separate because two very significant incidents happened during those years; moments that shaped me in ways I couldn't yet understand. One gave me hope. The other bound me in pressure. Together, they became the rhythm of my childhood: light and shadow, faith and fear, freedom and burden.

Looking back now, I see that pressure was not always what it seemed. To a child, it felt like a cage — rigid expectations, demands I could not meet. But hidden inside it was something else: love disguised as survival. And behind it all, God's hand; steady, though I could not yet see it. Sometimes His blessings come wrapped in joy, other times in responsibility, but both are meant to shape us for what lies ahead.

In those years, when the world outside mocked me and the world inside pressed down on me, hope had to be clung to wherever I could find it. Sometimes God places a small light in your path, just enough to keep you moving forward. For me, that light came in the form of a girl named Tien.

During those days, back at home in the apartment complex, I met her — another Vietnamese girl my age. I still remember the day she knocked on my door and asked if I wanted to play. My heart leapt. She looked like me. She understood.

Because in those years, that's exactly what she was: a small miracle wrapped in braids and laughter, sent to remind me that kindness could still find its way to me. When the world outside felt sharp and cruel, Tien's presence was like sunlight slipping through a crack in the blinds. She had a way of making ordinary afternoons feel like celebrations, the time I spent with her chased away the burdens I carried home from school.

That chance meeting grew into a friendship that lasted years, and our families grew close. On weekends, we gathered in each other's apartments, sharing food, laughter, and language. We traded dolls and secrets, made up dances in the courtyard, and told each other stories long after the adults had gone quiet. Her mother became like a second mother to me, her cooking filling the gaps where my own family could not.

I didn't know it then, but Tien would become one of the anchors of my childhood. With her, I wasn't the girl with the strange name or the too-short pants. I was simply me. And finally, for the first time in America, I didn't feel so alone.

But inside my home, another weight pressed down. My parents had made their expectations clear: one child would become a doctor, the other a lawyer. My brother — who declared at age five he wanted to be a lawyer — had the privilege of following his passion. I admired him for that. I envied him, too.

When I told my father I wanted to be a teacher, his face hardened. The disappointment in his eyes cut deeper than any words.

"No doctor? Then law school for you," he said in his broken English. Just like that, my dream crumbled.

Later, when I quietly requested information about graduate programs in psychology, the letters never made it past the mailbox. My father ripped them open and tore them apart in front of me. Piece by piece, my future shredded in his hands. I stood there devastated, understanding fully that to disobey him would mean dishonor. I felt trapped. Caught between the land of opportunity and the iron grip of my father's expectations.

Looking back now, I understand my father's choices in a way I could not as a child. To him, "doctor" and "lawyer" were not just professions; they were lifelines. They were shields of respect in a country that did not always welcome us. He had escaped back-breaking labor in Vietnam, and he was determined that his children would never stand behind a factory line or scrub floors in silence. In his mind, medicine and law were the two doors that could never be shut in America, the two titles that demanded recognition even from those who looked down on us. It wasn't cruelty that made him crush my letters to psychology programs; it was fear — fear that anything less would not be enough to protect me in this new world.

That was the paradox of becoming American. Freedom, but also pressure. Belonging, but also rejection. Opportunity, but also sacrifice.

And somewhere between fried chicken and pho, between shame in the schoolyard and hope at my family's dinner table, I learned my first lesson: adjustment is not about erasing who you are. It is about holding both worlds in your hands and learning how to live inside them both.

Back then, the pressure of my father's expectations felt like a cage. But now, with years behind me, I see it differently. God was using that very cage to train me, to strengthen me, to prepare me for the battles ahead. What once felt like imprisonment became, in time, the foundation of my calling.

Chapter Four: It begins at USC

"My *daughter*… my *lawyer*."

When my acceptance letter first arrived, my father held it like scripture. He ran his fingers over the words slowly, as if memorizing them. His chest swelled with pride, his voice booming to anyone who would listen.

"USC," he whispered.

I smiled for him, but inside I thought:

'Not *lawyer*. Teacher. Always *teacher.'*

It was one of those moments where joy and grief hold hands. My father's joy was undeniable. My grief had no place to speak. He bragged at dinners in the Vietnamese community, introducing me with shining eyes. I smiled, lowered my head, and let him have his joy. And I smiled, because how could I not? His joy was radiant. To him, the letter was a crown. To me, it was a verdict.

The first semester, I stood in front of my closet, tugging on a blazer with sleeves too long and shoulders that didn't quite fit.

"Do you think this looks okay?" I asked my brother.

He grinned. "It's fine, Nicole. Nobody cares about clothes at USC. They care about brains."

I didn't walk onto USC's campus with the confidence of someone who believed she belonged there. I walked onto the campus with a heart full of doubt. Everyone else seemed so sure of who they were, what they wanted. I, on the other hand, was chasing a dream that wasn't mine, hoping somewhere along the way, it might become one. But I felt both awe and displacement. The red-brick buildings stood tall and regal, draped in cardinal and gold banners. The lawns were manicured like something out of a magazine. Students bustled past me with new backpacks, new laptops, voices filled with stories of summer trips to Europe, ski cabins, or volunteer programs abroad. Their confidence was casual, like they had been born into it. I, on the other hand, carried the weight of my parents' escape across the ocean, their dreams pressed firmly onto my shoulders.

Still, I was determined to belong. I had to. I bought the sweatshirts, the t-shirts, even the license plate frame with "USC" blazing across it. I swiped my meal card at the campus eateries, gaining my freshman fifteen like everyone else. I lined up at the Starbucks outside the Levi Library, clutching a caramel macchiato as if it were a ticket into belonging. I studied under the harsh glow of the fourth floor's fluorescent lights, surrounded by the quiet hum of laptops and the faint scent of espresso. On the surface, I was playing the role of a USC student perfectly.

I even cheered at football games, pretending I understood the rules. Posed for photos with classmates whose parents spoke flawless English and whose futures already seemed assured. I laughed along when conversations turned to family vacations, nodding though I had nothing to contribute but the unspoken truth of my parents' boat ride across a dark sea.

I was living inside the American culture now, wrapped in its symbols of success — Starbucks cups, football games, crimson sweatshirts. But deep down, I knew I was living a story chosen for me, not by me.

My brother, always my anchor, was the one who urged me into the class that would change everything.

"Take Crime and Public Policy," he said one afternoon, nudging me. "The professor's a judge. He'll take care of us. You'll see."

I rolled my eyes. "I don't even want to be a lawyer."

"Doesn't matter. Just trust me."

I had to do something anyway. So, I took his suggestion.

Faith in Trials

The lecture hall was massive, seats rising like a theater. Students shuffled notebooks and laptops, the air buzzing with anticipation. Then he walked in — the professor, with invisible robes of authority draped across his shoulders. He didn't just teach. He challenged.

"Why do we punish?" he scrawled on the board, turning sharply to face us. "Revenge? Deterrence? Rehabilitation?" His eyes swept the room, daring us to answer.

Something in me stirred. Not excitement exactly but the way he spoke about justice, about law as more than rules — it was about people. Vulnerable people. Families. *Children.*

I didn't know it yet, but seeds were being planted. When class ended, my brother and I walked across the palm-lined path.

"Well?" he asked.

I shrugged, trying to mask the spark I felt. "He makes it sound… bigger than law. Like protecting people...children."

My brother grinned knowingly. "Told you."

Weeks later, the professor stopped me after class.

"You're Nicole Vo, right? Your brother told me about you."

I nodded nervously. "Yes, sir."

He studied me for a moment, then said, "You see the law as people, not just rules. That will make you a better lawyer."

I smiled politely.

Lawyer.

The word didn't fit me. It still felt like a coat I was forced to wear but I carried his words like a torch. And I won't lie, there were times when all this felt heavy. The new, big. And I would go home, in the quiet of my room, and I'd cry. I'd pray. I begged God to show me how His plan could possibly fit inside the prison of my father's expectations.

"Why me?" I whispered once. "Why not let me choose my own life?"

Silence. But not abandonment.

Jeremiah 29:11 (KJV) would return to me in those nights: ***"For I know the plans I have for you… plans to prosper you and not to harm you, plans to give you hope and a future."***

I clung to it, even when I didn't believe it at that point.

There were points when I told my brother, "I never wanted this. I wanted to teach. To work with children."

He looked at me with a steady kindness. "Maybe you still will. Just… in a different way."

I didn't understand what he meant then. But I carried those words with me.

Still, I kept walking forward. I studied hard, made connections, and tried to carve out a voice in a life I hadn't chosen. Each step felt like a tightrope — one foot balancing my father's pride, the other carrying the faint, buried dream of my own.

And as I walked that rope, I often wondered: how many others were doing the same? First-generation children, carrying both the gratitude of survival and the grief of lost dreams. Do they survive it? Will I?

When undergrad studies were completed and the day came to begin law school, I spotted my father's face beaming with happiness, pointing toward me, his chest swelling as he whispered to a neighbor, "That's my daughter. USC graduate. Soon, she will be lawyer."

I smiled and waved, playing the part he needed me to play.

Our family gathered with friends from the Vietnamese community. Over plates of food and polite laughter, my father introduced me again and again with the same phrase, "My daughter, the lawyer."

Faith in Trials

I knew the road wasn't over. USC had only been the beginning. The diploma wasn't the finish line; it was a doorway. And my father was already pointing me toward the next one.

"Law school," he said with certainty, as if it were destiny.

Chapter Five: Early Law School

And, law school was nothing like USC. If USC had been a wide ocean, law school was a storm at sea.

I still remember my very first day. Whittier's campus was small — maybe five buildings total — neat enough, but nothing compared to USC's regal, ornate grounds. I walked across cracked pavement and trimmed lawns, carrying books so heavy they bruised my shoulders. Inside, the hallways smelled faintly of old paper and burnt coffee. The walls were lined with portraits of tenured professors, each one solemn, stoic, their areas of expertise printed beneath their faces. Their eyes seemed to watch me, as if already measuring whether I belonged.

I didn't feel like I did. I felt lost, out of place, jealous even — watching classmates' eager faces, their buzz of excitement about being here. They wanted this. They longed for the late nights, the intellectual sparring, the rush of becoming a lawyer. I didn't. I longed instead for the classrooms at USC where chalk dust hung in the air, where psychology lectures had filled me with energy and wonder. Back then, I had walked into class with a spark. Here, I trudged in with dread.

It felt like a job. Punch in. Put in your hours. Memorize what they fed you. Take the exams. Check the boxes. Move toward the bar.

It was blurred together in exhaustion. Massive lecture halls packed with a hundred, sometimes two hundred students, everyone with their laptops open, typing furiously. The professors wasted no time on pleasantries; they dove straight into the material with no smiles, no warm introductions — just the law. Their voices droned like a code I wasn't fluent in: *precedent, torts, habeas corpus, mens rea.*

The Socratic method was merciless. Each day we were assigned three to four cases per class, which meant twelve cases on some days, each one demanding razor-sharp recall — facts, procedural history, rulings, reasoning. If you weren't prepared, you didn't just falter; you were humiliated. Professors ridiculed students in front of everyone, their unforgiving critiques leaving some red-faced, others near tears.

One afternoon, a professor's voice cut through the lecture hall: "Miss Vo, what is the holding in *Marbury v. Madison*?"

The room turned, eyes waiting. My chest tightened. I swallowed hard, words tumbling out half-correct, half-guess. A few students smirked. The professor raised an eyebrow but moved on. My cheeks burned the rest of class.

That night, I sat alone at my desk under the harsh glow of a lamp, flipping through the case again and again until the words blurred. "God," I whispered, "why am I here? I'm not cut out for this."

The thought came with a second wave: *Maybe it's me — maybe I'm not trying hard enough.* My chest tightened with a shame I could taste; I beat myself up for every missed volunteer, every hour I hadn't stayed late, every time I let my mind wander to chalkboards and instead of legal briefs. And then, almost as quickly, anger rose beneath the shame — why should I empty myself into something that has never been mine? Why pour my nights into a future that felt borrowed? The two feelings collided inside me like storm fronts: self-reproach on one side, stubborn protest on the other.

I closed the book, palms slick, and prayed:

You know I never wanted this. You know I wanted chalkboards and children, not case briefs and courtrooms. Help me see something You already see. Please don't let this misery be for nothing.

My life collapsed into textbooks. It was nothing like how you'd see in movies, it was crazy. Miss a single day of readings meant you were lost, drowning, unable to catch up. Three years stretched ahead of me like a cage. I had no social life, no reprieve except cafeteria food — greasy fries and vending machine snacks that stuck to me like regret. Some days I skipped meals altogether, my stomach growling in the middle of lectures.

Nicole Vo

Most days in law school, I drifted through the halls like a ghost; present, but not really alive. Thankfully, from time to time, on rare occasions, I was able to catch up with old friends from USC.

One day, a good friend of mine thought it would be a great idea to introduce me to his friend. It was an arranged date. I've never seen him around but agreed to the offer.

His name was Thang. The first thing I noticed about him was his sense of humor and sharp wittiness. He was very charming with a big heart. At our dinner date, he picked me up and took me to nice steakhouse. From there, the conversations were smooth and devoid of silence. We talked about our families, our upbringings, our hobbies, things we enjoyed doing, our hopes and dreams, etc... From there, the attraction was instant and we agreed on a second date.

And yet, even in that moment of lightness, my father's presence remained constant, anchoring me back to reality. Every night, he'd knock on my bedroom door, his voice brimming with care.

"How school? Are you keeping up?"

Each year completed was another step closer to his dream — the dream stolen from him in Vietnam, where war had robbed him of the chance to become who he wanted to be. Now, through me, he was living it. For him, my progress wasn't just academic. It was victory.

I smiled and nodded. "It's good." Then, almost shyly, I added, "I met someone, though."

His eyes widened, though his face remained composed. A few minutes later, he set down a small Vietnamese appetizer — something only he and I seemed to enjoy since I was a very young girl. We sat side by side and talked about *the guy.* He caught me smiling and pinched my arm, and I punched him back in protest. That only made us laugh harder. With his Budweiser in hand, we stayed up late while the house slept, talking about school, life, and yes, this new someone. He was curious, but never intrusive. Before heading to bed, he reminded me — gently but firmly — that his greatest fear was seeing me heartbroken. If I was hurt, he was hurt too. I smiled at him, knowing that was true.

Back at law school, it pushed me forward like a current too strong to fight. Professors saw my performance and appreciated it. Somehow, grades came back respectable. I amazed even myself—how could someone who hated this path appear competent on paper? At times, I would laugh at the irony but things weren't so bad. Law school was relentless, but Thang became this unexpected pocket of joy. A phone call between classes, coffee waiting for me at the end of the day, and a quick dinner before I returned to my studies. He made the weight I carried feel just a little lighter, reminding me that there was still life outside the walls of study rooms and exams. And suddenly, things weren't so bad I guess.

The first time I stepped into a courtroom as a law clerk, I expected to feel awe. My professor-turned-judge had taken me under his wings, patient with my fear, firm in his belief that I'd find my way. His courtroom was grand. He stood tall behind the bench, black robe commanding reverence. Attorneys moved with purpose, their arguments sharp, their cases meticulously prepared. I wore a suit, notebook in hand, trying to look like I belonged. At the end of the day, I would be exhausted and some nights when I wanted to quit, when the outlines blurred together and my head hit the desk in frustration, I'd find him, Thang, nudging me back up with words I didn't even know I needed: *"You've got this. You're going to be an incredible lawyer."* For someone who had always measured her worth in only being a lawyer, that kind of belief felt like a gift. Thang was also a successful businessman, confident in ways that seemed to balance my own doubts. For a young woman who had spent so much of her life trying to earn approval, his encouragement felt like relief. It felt like love.

One case stays with me still: a young man — barely older than I was — convicted of mayhem. A machete, a sliced ear, five years in prison. Just like that, his life narrowed to bars and numbers.

Day after day, I sat in court, watching trials unfold — attorneys clashing, jurors leaning in, witnesses trembling under the weight of their words. I told myself I was just overwhelmed, that the heaviness would pass. But beneath it, something darker was growing. The shouting, the sharp language, the pounding gavel — it all pressed in on me like walls closing too quickly. My chest tightened, breath catching in my throat. This wasn't awe. It was suffocation.

Before I knew what I was doing, I had fled into chambers, collapsing into a chair across from the judge, tears streaming.

"I can't do this," shaking my head. "This isn't me. I never wanted to be an attorney." The words startled even me. I had never dared to say them aloud.

The judge studied me for a long, quiet moment before answering, his voice steady. "Nicole… doubt doesn't disqualify you. It just makes you human."

Human. The word landed heavy, and strangely comforting. Enough to carry me back into the courtroom, though the ache lingered like an echo.

That night, I called Thang, my voice shaky as I recounted the day. Not long after, he showed up at my condo, took me out to have some sushi, insisting I put the books away for just one night.

"Future lawyers still need to eat," he teased, grinning as we enjoyed a California roll.

It was such a small thing, really. But it felt like sunlight breaking through — proof that maybe, just maybe, I could be both ambitious and human at the same time. With Thang, the tension of law's unrelenting weight found a counterbalance. It was a strange balance, but a needed one — his lightness against the grind, his humor against the silence of my books. He helped me find stability and peace after law school had overwhelmed me.

Soon after, I witnessed a child sexual abuse trial. I walked into the courtroom expecting the same rhythm I had grown numb to—motions, objections, legalese rattled off like it was a language only meant for lawyers. But that day was different. The prosecutor stood tall, his words carrying a fire I hadn't yet seen in law. It wasn't the fire of ambition or prestige. It was something purer, sharper—protection.

And then came the child. She couldn't have been more than eight or nine, her legs dangling off the witness chair, her voice trembling as she answered questions no child should ever have to speak aloud. I gulped down the lump in my throat. This was not a movie. This was real. The room was silent except for her small, halting words. I wanted to walk up, to shield her, to tell her she didn't have to do this.

I sat there, leaning forward, my chest heavy with a mix of grief and fury, I felt something I hadn't felt in three years of law school: purpose. For the first time, the law didn't look like codes, contracts, or casebooks. It looked like a shield. A voice. A chance to stand in the place where a child could not. My heart stirred in a way it hadn't since USC, since those psychology classes that once lit me up. Suddenly, the years of despair, the endless nights of reading cases I couldn't bring myself to care about, didn't feel wasted. Maybe God didn't abandon me; maybe He was leading me here.

It hit me then—the law could be more than my father's dream. It could be mine, too. Not because of the title, or the power, but because of the children. Vulnerable ones. Wounded ones. *My* children—the ones I had always longed to serve.

And in that moment, I stopped feeling like a warm body drifting through a life not my own. I felt alive. I felt called. That was my "ah-ha" moment. The first crack of light through the cage and once it opened, it could not be shut. I balanced this hit myself.

From then on, even when the courtroom pressed in on me—the shouting, the pounding gavel, the sharp words that left me breathless—I carried that moment inside me. The despair still surfaced, yes, but it no longer defined me. Because I had seen what the law could do when wielded for the most vulnerable. And I knew, finally, why I was here.

Law school graduation finally came. My father beamed with pride, carrying the badge of honor he had always longed for. To him, my diploma was the fulfillment of his dream. To me, it was something I was getting used to. To Thang, he had found his 'superwoman,' as he'd say.

Although, often times than most, I carried the weight of my father's expectations, but tucked inside my heart was something he couldn't see: the memory of a trembling child's voice, and the fire it lit in me. What I hadn't carried — at least not yet — was the thought of myself as anything other than a lawyer or a daughter.

Chapter Six: A Mother

We were already dating for two years before he proposed. The proposal was simple but sweet. A quiet dinner, nervous words, a ring held out in shaking hands. My heart said yes before my voice did. He wasn't perfect, but he felt steady, and after years of chasing approval and carrying expectations, steady felt like enough. There was not one reason to say no anyway. I loved how supportive he was of my dreams. He celebrated my late nights in the library, cheered me through exams, and told me over and over that he believed in the lawyer I was becoming, even in moments when I wasn't sure I believed in myself.

We married in November of 2004. I remember the air that day: cool but not cold, leaves just starting to scatter on the ground. And, weirdly enough, I never imagined myself in a white dress. Growing up, I was too busy trying to live up to my father's expectations, too weighed down by the invisible debts of our family's journey, to ever picture the details of a wedding. But somehow, there I was — standing before a mirror, lace pulled carefully across my shoulders, my father by my side.

His face softened. he looked at me not as the daughter who had to make him proud, but as a bride about to step into a life he believed would keep me safe.

The aisle stretched ahead of me like a promise. Family and friends filled the chairs, their faces glowing with expectation. When the music began and I took that first step, I remember thinking that maybe — just maybe — I had finally given my father what he wanted: proof that his sacrifices had secured me a future.

My parents were radiant that day. My mother fussed over my veil with tears in her eyes, prayers under her breath as though to cover me in blessing. My father walked me down the aisle with his shoulders straighter than I'd ever seen, pride woven into every step. For them, this was the American dream in flesh and blood: their daughter, educated, married, and secure. To them, it was as though every struggle, every sacrifice, had finally borne fruit.

The wedding was everything I imagined: glasses clinking, laughter rising, people giving heartfelt speeches about beginnings and blessings. My dress shimmered under the lights, my bouquet perfumed the air, and for one night I let myself believe in happily-ever-after.

In those early months, life unfolded like a dream. We were newlyweds learning the rhythm of "us" — burnt dinners that turned into laughter, arguments that ended with apologies, long nights talking about futures we hadn't yet built. I let myself breathe for the first time in years, convinced that I had finally found both love and safety.

And then, I became pregnant.

December 2004 — a date I'll never forget. It wasn't planned, but it didn't feel like an accident either. We were ecstatic, spinning conversations around names, colors for the nursery, what kind of parents we might be. I'd spend the day in court as a Deputy City Prosecutor, juggling misdemeanor cases, and come home to his hands on my stomach, whispering to the life inside me.

My mother glowed with joy, was already buying new baby clothes and making plans. My father's pride turned even sharper — his lawyer-daughter was now building a family of her own, the proof that he had given me both roots and wings. For a moment, it felt like we were all winning together.

For a while, married life felt like settling into a dream I had long chased. We painted walls in our new home, argued playfully over furniture, and cooked late dinners that rarely turned out like the recipes promised. We enjoyed planning get togethers and dinners at our new home with our friends and family. We loved hosting. Our home was theirs. We planned all the holidays such as Thanksgiving, Christmas, Chinese New Year, and Easter. We talked about children the way some people talk about vacations — with a light in our eyes, as though the future was guaranteed.

Faith in Trials

For a moment in time, it was everything I thought I wanted. But happiness has a fragile shell. And one ordinary day, it cracked.

I was back at work, my daughter just four months old, still adjusting after maternity leave, when my phone rang. It was him — my husband. His voice was stern, but wrong. Too careful. "It's important. We need to talk."

The words sent chills through me. "What's wrong? What's going on?" I asked, my heart already bracing.

What followed was a disclosure that shattered the life we had been building. Words that broke the air between us, leaving me in disbelief. Betrayal has a sound — it's the moment silence becomes unbearable, when tears stream faster than you can wipe them away. I wept openly, unable to stop, the room spinning around me. I do not wish to disclose what he said to me that changed everything between us to keep it private.

However, whatever we had, all of it was gone. The man I thought was my soulmate, my forever, had betrayed the trust we'd built.

The world I lived in yesterday was not the world I lived in today.

It took me days; even weeks to come to terms with what had happened until one day I finally told myself,

"You can't change what happened, but you can choose what happens next."

And so, I chose.

I chose to leave.

Not in haste, not in anger alone, but with clarity. My daughter became my compass. Protecting her was the first and only thought in my mind.

"I brought you into this world," I whispered as I held her close. "And I will not fail you."

Nicole Vo

I stayed longer than I should have — not because I couldn't see the truth, but because I wanted to believe in the story we had written. I wanted to believe love could outlast everything. But when Kylie came, clarity followed. I could not raise her in a house where shadows outweighed light.

So, there I was, twenty-something, a lawyer in training, a daughter still trying to balance old expectations — and suddenly, a mother. Alone.

Strength didn't come first; fear did. Fear of raising a child by myself. Fear of failing her the way I felt I had failed so many before. Fear of my family's judgment, who had sacrificed everything for me, only to see me stumble in the one thing they thought would secure my future.

But in the quiet of those nights, when it was just me and the sound of her breathing, something else rose up to meet the fear: faith. And then I said to myself. "When you remember where God brought you from, you will never stop doubting where God can take you." I began to understand that motherhood was not another role to perform for my father or for the world. It was a sacred trust, a gift from God Himself, who knew my breaking point and met me there. And in the back of mind my, I heard a voice telling me." Every single thing that has happened in your life is preparing you for something that's meant to come."

Chapter Seven: Swearing In Ceremony

Confidence doesn't come all at once. For me, it came in fragments—fleeting moments when fear gave way to something steadier, something fierce. The morning of the swearing-in ceremony, I stood before my bedroom mirror, my suit pressed until every crease was sharp, the fabric clinging like a second skin. The official title wasn't just a symbol of pride or responsibility—it was the weight of every sacrifice, every tear, every night I'd spent piecing myself back together after my marriage shattered. Kylie's soft laughter drifted from the next room, a reminder of the future I was fighting for, but also of the wreckage I carried. My heart was broken, still raw from the divorce, and the absence of my ex-husband ached like a bruise. But I had my father. And that was all that mattered.

I whispered a verse to my reflection, my voice barely steady: ***"Trust in the Lord with all your heart and lean not on your own understanding. In all your ways, submit to him, and he will make your paths straight."*** Proverbs 3:5-6 (KJV). The words felt like a lifeline, but doubt clawed at me. *What if I fail her? Fail him? Fail myself?* The official title felt heavy, as if it might pull me under. I gripped my DA pin tighter, willing myself to believe I was enough.

"You know what you want now," I murmured, but the words cracked, fragile against the storm inside.

Los Angeles traffic was merciless, a snarl of horns and chaos that mirrored my nerves as I drove to pick up my father. Kylie stayed home with my mother, her tiny hands probably wrapped around a toy, oblivious to the mountain on my shoulders. My father sat quietly beside me, his hands folded in his lap, but his joy radiated, filling the car like a heartbeat. I glanced at him, catching his smile—too wide to contain, cracking through his usual stoicism. It reminded me of our late-night talks about law school, work, life, when he'd listen with that same quiet pride. When he'd heard about the divorce, he was shocked, like everyone else. But when I told him why, he just nodded, his silence a shield.

Today, though, his fingers tapped lightly against his leg, betraying his nerves. He was more nervous than I was, I realized. This day wasn't just mine; it was his too. Years of lectures, pressure, and dreams had funneled into this moment, a shared victory born of his sacrifices.

The hall at headquarters was a cathedral of hushed anticipation, the air thick with the restless buzz of proud families and nervous peers. Rows of new attorneys sat stiffly, some with bouncing knees, others grinning with a confidence I envied. The polished floor gleamed under the lights, reflecting the flags that loomed like silent judges. The weight of the moment pressed against my ribs—grand, official, suffocating. My throat tightened, a wild urge to bolt screaming in my veins. *What if I'm not good enough?* The question whispered through me, sweat tickling my forehead. I gulped, my breath shallow, until my eyes found him.

My father sat near the front, his smile so wide it could have lit the entire hall. Our gazes locked, and everything inside me stilled. For once, he didn't look critical or demanding—just proud, fulfilled, as if his life's mission was complete. I could almost hear him whisper, *"Ni. My daughter. Lawyer. District Attorney."* That look burned away my doubt, tethering me to the truth: I wasn't just his daughter carrying his expectations. I was his equal, stepping into a fire he'd fought to give me. I held back a tear, my heart swelling with a love too big for words.

"Nicole Lai Vo," the announcer's voice boomed, clear and deliberate, slicing through the silence.

My name—*Lai*, the syllable I'd once flinched at, the one kids had twisted into taunts until I wanted to erase it- echoed in the hall like a reclamation. My palms were slick, my legs unsteady as I rose, each step to the stage a thunderclap in my ears. The room blurred, faces dissolving into a haze of expectation. My hands shook as I reached for the pin placed on my lapel.

Did they notice? I couldn't tell. All I felt was its weight, anchoring me to this moment, to this truth: I was here. I belonged.

I sank back into my seat, my fingers brushing the pin, tracing its shape to confirm it was real. The doubts didn't vanish—they never do—but they no longer owned me. I was 80% certain, and that was enough. My mind flashed to that first child trial, the little girl's shaky voice, her small hands clutching the witness stand. Her courage had broken me open, lit a fire I couldn't extinguish. If I could carry her story, hold her pain without shattering, I could carry this too. I didn't have to be perfect. I just had to be present.

This wasn't just a ceremony, a name announced, a pin handed over. It was monumental—a line between before and after, between the young lawyer chasing a dream that wasn't hers and the Officer of the Court standing tall. I was ready to say it aloud: *Nicole Vo, Deputy District Attorney for the People.* The pride burned fierce, but alongside it came a heaviness I couldn't ignore. This wasn't just an honor. It was power. And power meant responsibility—to Kylie, to the children I'd sworn to protect, to the father whose sacrifices had carried me here.

The applause roared as the ceremony ended, families surging forward, their voices a tide of joy. I found my father in the crowd, and we stood shoulder to shoulder, not just as family, but as two souls who understood the cost of this calling. His eyes held a pride too deep for words, and mine burned with a resolve I was only beginning to claim. I wanted to say, *I will make you proud.* But the words stayed inside—they weren't needed. His nod, steady and sure, said it all. I smiled, my heart full.

Later, we drove to Chinatown and sat across from each other, two steaming bowls of noodles between us. He barely touched his food, too full of pride to eat. I didn't mind. Just being there, sharing that quiet victory, was enough. Between bites, he spoke, his voice thick with emotion. "When we first came to America, we were powerless," he said. "We stumbled over English, felt out of place in a culture that wasn't ours. But now—with a successful business and two children who became attorneys—we finally feel some power. We no longer feel inferior." His eyes glistened with tears as he looked at me. "I'm proud of you."

Those words landed like a balm, soothing wounds I hadn't realized still ached. This day wasn't just about a pin or a title. It was about every version of me—the daughter of immigrants, the child who'd learned English word by word, the girl who'd shrunk under her own name, the mother fighting for her daughter's future. They were all here, walking together, claiming their place. And as I took a deep breath, my hand brushing the pin on my suit, I knew: this was my calling, my fire, my purpose. I was ready.

Chapter Eight: The Badge Ceremony

The first few months as a "baby DA" thrusted me into a role that felt both exhilarating and overwhelming. The title—shorthand for a new Deputy District Attorney in Los Angeles—carried a weight of authority I was only beginning to grasp.

As a Deputy DA, I was an officer of the court, tasked with representing the People of the State of California, prosecuting crimes, and seeking justice for victims in courtrooms where every word could tip the scales. It meant wielding the power to hold wrongdoers accountable, to stand for those who couldn't—children, survivors, the vulnerable—while navigating a system that demanded precision, resilience, and ethical clarity. The label marked me as untested, a newcomer in the Los Angeles District Attorney's Office, yet it also placed me within a legacy of justice, a mantle I was learning to carry.

Assigned to three rotations in my first year, I dove into preliminary hearings and misdemeanor jury trials, each case a crucible for my voice, my resolve. I was finding my footing, speaking with growing authority as "Nicole Vo, Deputy DA for the People." But beneath the rush of this new role, a shadow was gathering, dark and unyielding.

Three months into my first jury trial assignment, my world shattered. My father—the man whose pride had anchored me, whose sacrifices across an ocean had paved my path—was diagnosed with Stage 4 lung cancer. The doctor's words hit like a sledgehammer: six to eight months to live. I remember I sat frozen in the sterile hospital room, the air thick with antiseptic and dread, as the prognosis sank in. My heart pounded, refusing to accept it.

Six to eight months? It couldn't be real.

This was my father, the unyielding force who'd survived a war, a prison camp, a desperate escape on a wooden boat. He was my best friend and hero. A man that was supposed to be indestructible, the one who'd always be there, nodding with quiet pride. My hands trembled, my chest so tight I could barely breathe. I wanted to scream, to beg God to rewind time, to give me just one more year, one more day with him. The thought of losing him; of facing this world without his steady gaze; was a knife twisting in my gut.

I pictured Kylie growing up without her grandfather, his stories of Vietnam fading into silence. The future I'd imagined, the one where he'd see me rise as a lawyer, crumbled like ash. I clung to his hand, his skin thinner than I remembered, and whispered,

"Please, don't go. " I could barely utter. But as always, his eyes, still fierce despite the pain, held mine, as if saying,

"Keep going, Ni. Don't stop."

Then what followed was a blur. My father wasn't getting any better. The doctors' believed hospice was the next step for him. We decided as a family to do hospice at our house where he could pass in peace. Our house was filled with family members from both sides of the family, many of whom flew in from out of state to pay their last respect. I was always by his side making sure that I did not miss any last moments with him. Suddenly, he looked at me, and I looked at him, we nodded in agreement and he took his last breath.

Days later both families prepared for the elaborate celebration of life that was to follow. At the graveyard, hundreds of people gathered. The air was heavy with incense and grief. My father followed the Buddhist religion. Monks walked around his coffin chanting that his spirit leave his body towards enlightenment. The monks were made aware of the close relationship we had. In order for his spirit to leave his body, the monks did not allow me to see his casket being lowered to the ground. I was directed to leave the site of the burial, and was allowed to return until dirt had covered his coffin. I moved back, standing near my car, my legs weak, watching as the earth claimed him. The creak of the ropes, the soft thud of dirt, the finality of it all—it carved itself into me, a wound that would never fully heal.

Faith in Trials

The badge ceremony arrived weeks later, a moment that should have been a triumph but felt like a wound. I stood before my mirror, my suit pressed sharp. It was supposed to mark my full acceptance as a Deputy DA, a symbol of the battles I'd won in courtrooms. Instead, it was a reminder of the one battle I'd lost. I wanted to honor him, to carry his pride, but all I felt was a bone-deep loneliness, a daughter unmoored without her father's gaze.

The hall at the Arboretum and Botanic Garden thrummed with celebration—families whispering, peers fidgeting with nervous energy, the air thick with new beginnings. I sat among them, a ghost in my own skin. I can't do this without him. My eyes searched the crowd for a face that wasn't there, his absence a sharper pain than any I'd known. I remember celebrating that moment- joyous yet somber- alone. Kylie was not there. My mom and brother were not there. My aunts and uncles were not there. They were required to be at my dad's wake. I had no one to hug. I had no one to take pictures with. The joy of cheering families only deepened my isolation, leaving me adrift in a sea of celebration.

"Nicole Lai Vo," the announcer's voice rang out again, clear and final.

My hands trembled as I took the badge, its weight pulling at me like an anchor. The applause was distant, muffled by the roar of my grief. This was supposed to be our moment—his daughter, his lawyer, his legacy. I looked in the crowd again, tears blurring my eyes. I don't know what I was looking for. Maybe, somehow, God would have mercy on me, I would see my father's face.

But I didn't.

Instead, I stood alone, clutching the badge he'd never see. I rushed out as soon as my name was called, tears burning my eyes, my heart racing to reach his week-long wake—a traditional gathering for the firstborn son of the Vo family. I had to be there, to honor him, even as his absence shattered me.

Nicole Vo

Outside the venue, the world blurred through my tears. I stumbled toward my car, the weight of the day crushing me, each step heavier than the last. I was breathless and all I wanted to do was cry.

Then, a flicker of movement stopped me cold. A small bird—tiny, delicate, with soft brown feathers and eyes like polished beads—landed directly by my foot. Birds don't do that. They scatter; they flee.

But this one didn't. It stood there, unafraid, its gaze meeting mine with a quiet, knowing stillness. My breath caught, and in that fleeting moment, I knew. It was him. My father, proud and unwavering, celebrating my badge in spirit. The air stilled, the world falling silent as if God Himself had paused it. The ache in my chest lifted, replaced by a warmth that felt like his hand on my shoulder, his nod, his smile. He was here, woven into the mystery of this tiny creature, telling me I wasn't alone.

That bird became more than a moment; it became a sacred symbol; a lifeline etched into my soul. It would reappear in the years ahead, outside courtrooms during grueling trials, perched on branches when despair threatened to swallow me, or fluttering past my window in the silence of sleepless nights. Each time, it carried my father's pride, God's presence, a whisper of faith over fear. It was as if they had conspired to mark my path with this tiny messenger, a reminder that love and strength endure beyond loss, beyond death. The bird was my father's voice when I couldn't hear him, God's promise when I felt forsaken. It became my anchor, a sign that I could face any trial—because I was never truly alone.

In that instant outside the venue, I wiped my tears, my fingers brushing the badge in my pocket. Grief and loneliness gave way to a fragile comfort, a certainty that they were walking with me. The badge wasn't just a title or a piece of metal—it was his legacy, my calling, a fire I would carry for him, for Kylie, for the children I'd sworn to protect as a Deputy DA. I took a deep breath, the bird still watching, and stepped forward into the life I was meant to live.

Chapter Nine: Voices in the Courtroom

A good friend once told me, 'The future is not something you wait for. It's something you create.'

Every new prosecutor remembers their first trial. For some, it's a stolen car or a bar fight, a single defendant and a handful of witnesses. Mine began that way too — smaller cases, one victim, one file, one courtroom. They taught me the mechanics: how to question a witness, how to present evidence, how to keep my own nerves steady while a jury watched. But nothing prepared me for the avalanche that would become my first major felony sexual abuse case.

It started like any other file; a custody case, one child, one suspect. At least, that's what I thought. I sat across from Judy, my investigating officer, flipping through the report, when she told me another disclosure had surfaced in a neighboring city. A second child. Then a third. Before I could even steady myself, names kept appearing like shadows out of nowhere. By the time we were done, there were six. Six children, none of them related, none of them with reason to know about each other — yet all pointing to the same man.

The suspect was the kind of person you'd never expect: an uncle, a football coach, a trusted family friend. The kind of man parents welcomed into their homes, the kind who slipped under every guard because trust had already been given to him. He had groomed each child carefully; the gifts, the laughs, the whispered lies of "this is normal" and "you won't get in trouble." He gave them drugs to dull their fear and videotaped his crimes as though preserving a library of destruction.

I can still see the first boy who sat in my office. He could barely speak. His eyes stayed fixed on the floor, his small hands twisting together as though holding in something too painful to share. I handed him a sheet of paper and a pen.

"Draw whatever you want," I told him gently. "You're safe here."

Minutes passed in silence until lines began to form. A child, a man, and beside them, a sharp object. I leaned closer.

"Help me understand? Tell me what this means?" I asked softly.

His lips quivered, but the words came: "That's the screwdriver he used when he hurt me."

I felt the air leave the room. But I didn't let my face flinch, not once. In that moment, my job was to be steady, to be the anchor he could cling to while naming horrors no child should ever have to describe. Later, that piece of paper would become evidence, but in that moment, it was a lifeline.

The case grew heavier with each child's disclosure. Some spoke haltingly, others with a flood of words they had been waiting years to release. Ages ranged from six to thirteen. One told me how he had been raped in the shower moments before police knocked on the door. Another recalled being forced to watch videos of himself. Each story was a different shard of the same shattered truth.

In court, the weight of it all became undeniable. I remember standing at the prosecutor's table, the jury staring as one small witness after another walked to the stand.

"The People call Joey."

"The People call Christopher."

Each name echoed through the courtroom, each child's testimony another wave against the defense. I watched the jurors' faces shift from disbelief to heartbreak. Their eyes asked the same unspoken question: How could one man cause this much devastation?

The answer sat a few feet away, silent at the defense table.

Trials are not TV dramas. They are long, grueling marathons of testimony, evidence, objections, and procedure. But this case was different. Every word mattered because behind every word was a child. And though I was the one speaking in court, I knew I was standing for voices that had once been silenced by fear.

When the verdicts came, they came one after another — guilty, guilty, guilty. Twenty-six counts in all. The sentence: 126 years to life in state prison. A number so large it might as well have been written in stone. He would never walk free again.

I thought I would feel relief, and I did — but what surprised me was the fire that burned deeper than relief. This case had not scared me away. It had done the opposite. For the first time in my career, I knew with absolute clarity: this was my calling.

Some prosecutors in my unit couldn't stomach cases like this. They would go home, shower, try to scrub the images out of their minds. For me, it was different. I loved children too much to turn away. I had once dreamed of being a teacher, but God had written a different plan. He had placed me here — not in a classroom, but in a courtroom, protecting children in a way I never could have imagined.

Even now, years later, I can still hear their voices. I can still see the drawings, the trembling hands, the courage it took for them to speak. Those memories never fade. And I don't want them to. Because they remind me why I fight.

That first big case taught me that justice is not abstract. It is a child finally exhaling because someone believed them. It is a jury rising to say, "We hear you." It is a predator led away in chains so he can never touch another life.

And for me, it was the moment fear gave way to purpose.

Looking back, I know it was God's hand that steadied me in that courtroom. Left on my own, the weight of those children's stories would have crushed me. But every time I felt the urge to break, He gave me strength. Every time doubt whispered that I wasn't enough, He reminded me why I was there.

Nicole Vo

I once thought I had failed because I never became the teacher I dreamed of being. But God showed me that protecting children didn't require a classroom — it required courage, faith, and the willingness to stand in the gap when no one else could.

I will never forget the look on the jurors' faces as each child took the stand. Shock. Disbelief. Sorrow. And finally, conviction. It was as though God Himself had opened their eyes to see the truth, to feel the weight of innocence lost, and to rise up in defense of the vulnerable. Their verdict was more than a legal decision — it was a declaration that evil had been exposed, and justice would prevail.

That trial became my altar, a place where I saw clearly: this was more than a career. This was my calling.

Chapter Ten: A Marriage That Should Have Never Been

"When you pass through the waters, I will be with you;

and when you pass through the rivers, they will not sweep over you.

When you walk through the fire, you will not be burned;

the flames will not set you ablaze." – *Isaiah 43:2 (KJV)*

There are seasons in life that feel like wilderness — long stretches of quiet where God seems to whisper instead of speak. That was the season I found myself in before I remarried.

Years of single motherhood made me resilient but also weary in places I didn't speak of out loud. My days were filled with work, cases, and deadlines, and my nights belonged to Kylie — bedtime stories, gentle laughter, the soft rhythm of her breathing as she fell asleep beside me. When the house grew still, I would sit at the edge of my bed with my Bible open, running my fingers along verses that had carried me through darker storms.

Sometimes I'd close my eyes and whisper, *"Lord, I've done the hard part. I've walked through the valley. When will peace come?"*

It wasn't that I was chasing romance — I was chasing rest. I wanted to feel safe enough to exhale again. To have someone beside me who understood what it meant to lead, to protect, to build. I longed for stability not out of weakness, but because I had spent too many years being the strong one.

There is a certain fatigue that comes from holding everything together alone — paying bills, carrying emotional weight, keeping faith alive. I had mastered independence, but somewhere deep down, I missed partnership. I missed having someone to pray with, to dream with.

I told myself I wasn't desperate for love; I was simply ready for companionship that felt safe and grounded in God.

When he entered my life, he seemed to appear in answer to that prayer. He spoke of faith, family, and building something lasting. He seemed mature — someone with life experience and drive. Someone who understood what it meant to start over.

I remember one night, sitting on the porch with a cup of tea, watching the sky darken, and thinking, *maybe this is what God meant when He said He would restore what the locusts have eaten.*

I wanted to believe that after all the heartache — the losses, the first divorce, the nights of silent tears — God was finally giving me a new beginning. A chance to rewrite the story.

Friends told me I deserved happiness. My mother said I had spent enough time alone. Even my own heart began to soften at the thought of family dinners, holidays filled with laughter, and a father figure for Kylie.

The more we talked, the more I let myself hope. He spoke the right words — words that echoed everything I'd prayed for: faith, unity, stability. I told myself this was divine timing. After all, hadn't I waited long enough?

"God, if this is from You," I prayed one night, *"then bless it. Let this be the man who brings calm, not chaos. Let this be the home where laughter replaces fear."*

I wanted to believe that stability could be found in shared dreams — in building a family rooted in love and faith.

And so, with the kind of faith only hope can produce, I said yes to a new chapter. I walked into marriage believing I was finally stepping into the peace I had prayed for.

Faith in Trials

When I remarried, I thought I was finally stepping into the peace I had prayed for. After years of trials, loss, and single motherhood, I longed for stability — not perfection, just something steady.

Stability, to me, meant safety. It meant a partner who was grounded in his faith, who had life experience, and who wanted to build a home that felt like harmony. I dreamed of a family table where laughter replaced loneliness, where Kylie would have siblings to grow up with and a father figure who would protect her the way my own father once protected me.

I wanted holidays filled with warmth and color; birthdays, family vacations, the smell of cinnamon and laughter echoing through our home. I wanted to create the kind of life that reminded me of God's goodness after so much pain.

And at first, it seemed like I had found it.

The early months were soft. Dinners at home, helping the children with their homework, winding down in the evenings as a family. I told myself, *This is what peace must feel like.* After years of holding the weight of the world in the courtroom, I wanted to come home and simply exhale.

But peace built on fragile ground cannot last.

When we moved in together, I began to see small fractures — cracks I wanted to ignore. They didn't come all at once; they whispered. The first came in the way he spoke to his children — harshly, with words that broke instead of built. I would see their faces fall, their shoulders stiffen, and something inside me would twist.

He said he loved them, and I believe he did, but love without gentleness can wound deeply. I would lie awake at night thinking of their tears, telling myself I'd never allow Kylie to be spoken to that way.

At first, I tried to make excuses. *He's just stressed. He's been through so much. He doesn't mean it.* But the excuses grew thin as the pattern grew clear.

The second fracture came in how he treated his employees — the same sharpness, the same unpredictable temper. People came and went through his company like shadows through a revolving door. I remember wondering why no one ever stayed long.

And then, slowly, that tone — the one I had witnessed from afar — turned toward me.

At first, it was small things. Constant questions. Repeated phone calls while I was at work:

"Where are you?"

"Who are you talking to?"

"Who did you have lunch with?"

"When are you coming home?"

I told myself it was care, not control. But care should feel safe — not suffocating.

His moods swung like a pendulum. One hour, he'd tell me I was the best thing that had ever happened to him. The next, he'd accuse me of betrayal, his words slicing deep and fast. I had prosecuted cases like these before — the patterns of control, the slow erasure of confidence — but living inside it felt like walking through fog. I was walking on eggshells.

I began to shrink without realizing it. I spoke less, smiled less, laughed less. I tiptoed around moods, learning to measure peace by silence instead of joy.

And yet, I still prayed.

"Lord, I asked You for stability. Is this what it looks like? If I'm wrong, show me. Please, give me wisdom."

Faith in Trials

The answer didn't come immediately. God's silence can sometimes feel like absence, but looking back, I know He was watching, waiting for me to see what He already knew.

When I suggested counseling, I hoped it would help us find the root of our storms. We attended a few sessions, and I watched in quiet disbelief as his anger filled the room — shouting, pacing, the kind of rage that chills the air. I remember the therapist's eyes darting to mine in fear. When the session ended, she asked to speak to me privately.

Her words were steady but urgent: "Nicole, he meets every marker for borderline personality disorder. You need an exit plan — for your safety and your daughter's."

That night, I sat alone in my car, the parking lot lights washing over the steering wheel. I looked up the disorder she'd mentioned, and as I read, I felt the pieces of my life rearranging themselves into a truth I could no longer deny. Every symptom, every shift, every word I had ignored — it was all there, printed in black and white.

Still, leaving wasn't instant. Love and faith can make you linger in hope. I remembered his past pain, the stories of his own childhood abuse. The prosecutor in me understood trauma; the healer in me wanted to rescue him from it.

But you can't save someone who doesn't want saving.

Over time, even Kylie began to sense it. She was still so young — five, maybe six — yet children have instinct adults sometimes lose. I could see the unease in her eyes, the way she stayed quiet when he entered a room.

One night, after he raised his voice again, something in me finally broke open. I saw Kylie watching from the hallway, her small hands gripping her iPad. I felt her fear as if it were my own.

That was the night I drew the line in my heart.

If he ever lays a hand on me, we're leaving.

And when that moment came — when anger turned to touch, and touch became a boundary crossed — I didn't hesitate. I gathered my strength, my child, and the remnants of my peace, and we left.

As we stepped outside, his voice followed, sharp and final:

"You'll pay for this."

But I had already paid enough.

When we got into the car, my hands trembled against the steering wheel. I felt Kylie's small hand on my arm.

"Here, Mom," she said softly, unlocking her iPad. "I'll help us find an apartment."

Her courage steadied me more than any verse ever could in that moment. I started the car, whispering through tears,

"God, guide me. Don't let me be afraid. Help me start over."

I didn't look back.

I filed for divorce two days later. In response, he retaliated by filing a civil lawsuit against me, seeking $2 million in damages. Sadly, he knew the lawsuit was frivolous, but he filed it anyway. I was stunned by his actions. It was obvious he knew I didn't have that kind of money. In my heart, I believed it was his way of trying to force me back to him. His behavior was consistent with patterns often seen in abusive relationships.

The lawsuit forced me to hire an attorney to defend myself. It came at a significant financial cost, but I was determined to stand my ground. After six months of demanding discovery and him failing to do so, I demanded my trial. Faced with that reality, he ultimately had no choice but to dismiss the case.

Starting over was both familiar and foreign. I had rebuilt before — after my first divorce, after my father's death — but this time was different. This time, I wasn't just surviving loss; I was reclaiming peace.

Faith in Trials

In the months that followed, I refused to let fear take root. I reminded myself daily of Romans 8:28 — ***"And we know that God works all things for good for those who love Him."***

That verse became my anchor.

Yes, I was exhausted. I had uprooted Kylie too many times for her short age. But I was also filled with a determination I didn't know I still had.

Each morning, I woke before dawn, prayed over my coffee, and thanked God for another chance to build a safe home. I made a vow — one I still keep — that every year, I'd take Kylie on a "mommy and me" vacation. A new island, a new adventure, a memory of joy to replace what fear had stolen.

We've seen the Caribbean sunsets together, the turquoise water reflecting light so pure it felt like redemption. In those quiet moments — sand beneath our feet, waves whispering against the shore — I'd look at her and think, *This is stability.* Not in a man. Not in a house. But in the bond between mother and daughter, protected by God's hand.

Sometimes I still catch myself wondering what would have happened if I'd ignored my instincts, if I had stayed for one more promise. But then I remember what peace feels like — real peace — and I know I made the right choice.

I no longer chase the idea of a perfect family. My definition of stability has changed.

It means being emotionally and financially whole on my own.

It means trusting my intuition without apology.

It means knowing that failure doesn't define me — faith does. It means I am responsible for my own joy, my own safety, my own life.

And above all, it means believing that God's love is not found in chaos, but in calm.

There are still days when I think about that chapter of my life and feel a faint ache — not regret, but remembrance. I don't resent the woman I was then. I honor her. She did the best she could with what she knew. She stayed until she understood she was worth more.

I don't see weakness when I look back; I see growth. I see the hand of God pulling me out of waters that once threatened to drown me.

And even now, when doubt whispers — *What if it happens again? What if you're alone forever?* — I answer with the quiet certainty of someone who has already walked through fire and come out unburned:

"The Lord is my strength and my shield; my heart trusts in Him, and He helps me." — Psalm 28:7 (KJV)

I didn't know what the next chapter of my story would've held. Maybe it's peace. Maybe it's purpose. Maybe it's simply learning to rest in what is.

But I know this: I am not afraid anymore.

Because I have walked through the storm, and I am still standing.

Because I have seen fear lose its grip.

Because I have learned that faith — real faith — isn't proven in safety; it's proven in survival.

And for the first time in a long time, I can breathe again.

Chapter Eleven: The Wrath That Came

"Be still, and know that I am God."

— Psalm 46:10 (JKV)

Two years had passed since I last heard from my ex.

If I started writing down every moment that felt like a task — every second I was too weak to stand but forced myself up anyway, for myself, for my daughter — this book would never end.

The divorce papers had long been filed away, and with them, the version of me that once begged for peace. I was rebuilding, slowly, clumsily, but with purpose. My daughter and I were learning how to exist as two halves of one small world, fitting the broken pieces together as best we could. Every day was work. Mornings were heavy, nights heavier but she made even the hard parts feel bearable. As dramatic as it sounds, the sun really did shine brighter when she was near.

At work, things were relentless. There was no shortage of pain in my line of work; the kind that crawls into your bones if you let it. I had trained myself to build a wall between home and courtroom.

Every victim's voice, every photo, every testimony, it all clung to me. But I couldn't afford to let the darkness follow me home. I had a little girl waiting there, and she deserved laughter, not leftovers of my sorrow. So, I built an invisible line; work stayed on one side, motherhood on the other. Maybe that was my way of protecting her, of keeping even the faintest shadow of this world from touching her innocence.

It was around that time I met Tim. We worked within the same justice system; he investigated the kind of cases I prosecuted. Our paths had crossed in court corridors, sometimes in whispered consultations over files, but never closely enough to call it fate. Until one day, it was.

I remember sitting in the worship center as the Pastor spoke. A moment of clarity and discernment came from the Lord.

"You will call him."

My heart jumped into my throat.

"No, Lord," I whispered under my breath. "What if he's married?"

I left it at that or at least I tried to. But later that day, while wandering the aisles of Bed Bath & Beyond with my daughter, it came again, louder this time, almost playful in its persistence:

"Nicole, you will call him."

I sighed — a surrender wrapped in defiance.

"Fine, Lord. I'll do it. But only on my terms. If he doesn't respond in ten minutes, I'll take that as my sign that he's with someone else." The irony of this story is that Tim had asked me out for coffee two years earlier, but I declined. At the time, I was married to my ex-husband.

It sounds silly now — giving God an ultimatum — but in that moment, I needed some kind of control. So, one simple text later, my thumb trembling over the "send" button, I hit it and walked away from my phone.

Ten minutes later, it rang. God sure works in mysterious ways!

When I answered, his voice was warm, familiar, like a door I hadn't realized I'd kept locked suddenly opening. We talked for hours that night, about everything and nothing. He asked me to lunch. A few days later, dinner. I told myself it was casual, two old colleagues catching up but even then, deep down, I knew something had shifted.

Meeting Tim felt like breathing fresh air after years underground. My last relationship made me fear men. But he was different. He carried peace like other people carry perfume; quietly, naturally, leaving traces of calm wherever he went.

He listened. He really listened.

We dated for four years. During that time, we traveled across the country — New York, San Francisco, and Hawaii — and even ventured to the islands of Turks and Caicos, my happy place.

The laughter and friendship we shared became the foundation of our newfound love. I can share my thoughts with him without fear of being judged. Over time, he became my best friend and my rock. He is a man of integrity and faith — a God-fearing man. He's someone who truly understands me. He shows patience and forgiveness so effortlessly; the kind I had prayed for over a very long time, and in many ways, he reminds me of my dad. He fills a space in my heart that felt empty for so long.

When I told him about the past and of the nights I didn't sleep, the weight of the guilt that wasn't mine, he didn't interrupt or try to fix it. He just let me unravel. There were times I would cry so hard I could barely breathe, and he'd just hold me, his silence saying what words couldn't. He reminded me that strength didn't always look like standing tall. Sometimes it was just showing up, even when your knees shook. With him, I started to believe that maybe life wasn't done being kind to me.

Then came February 24, 2016 — the day the ground shifted again.

A missed call.

A voicemail. How did he manage to get a hold of my new cell phone?

His voice — my ex's — soft, polite, eerily calm. He said he harbored no grudges. That he wished me well. That he blamed himself for what went wrong. For a brief second, I smiled. Maybe he'd finally realized his mistakes. Maybe this was closure. I even whispered a small prayer, thanking God for letting him find peace.

Until it wasn't peace at all. He hunted me down and managed to find out where I lived.

The next week, he started showing up again. Unannounced. Uninvited.

Once, he left my purse outside my apartment door; my old things, neatly cleaned, mended, polished like a twisted offering. Inside was a note, his handwriting instantly recognizable:

"Let's meet for drinks. Let's bury old wounds."

It was the kind of message that sounded harmless to anyone else, but to me, it was loaded. A memory of hands that gripped too tight. Words that sliced under the guise of love.

Then another voicemail. His tone was still soft, almost gentle — but beneath it, something dark coiled. He was still trying to control me. Still refusing to let me go. I thought I was finally free. That God had answered the prayer I'd whispered a hundred times in the dark. The wounds were still there, but at least they'd stopped bleeding. I was learning to breathe again, to live without that constant ache in my chest. And yet, every time my phone rang from an unknown number, my stomach would knot. My hands would shake and my heart pounded uncontrollably.

Fear, I learned, doesn't need logic, it just needs memory.

Sometimes, I'd stare at the screen until it stopped ringing. Often times, I just let it go to voicemail.

Then, one quiet afternoon in late 2016, my phone rang again.

"Irvine Police Department."

Two words — that's all it took for my body to freeze. My throat went dry. My mind raced through every possible reason they could be calling me.

Is my daughter okay?

Is this about a case?

I could've lived with either of those. But no — it was about him. "Theft and forgery," they said. "Video evidence. Photos." And just like that, I was no longer a bystander — I was implicated.

My voice came out trembling, but steady enough: "Please… I want nothing to do with him. Whatever he's done, leave me out of it. I divorced him three years ago."

The officer's voice was professional, almost bored, but my gut knew better. Fear has a way of training the soul, you start to sense the storm before it breaks. He couldn't control me anymore, so now he'd try to ruin me. For a while, it went quiet again. I convinced myself it was over. The drama died down. I started to breathe normally. I even laughed again without flinching at my phone.

By April 2017, four months after my last contact with my ex, I'd managed to hold myself together. Barely. My calendar was full, and that was good; motion had always been my medicine. So, when my supervisor asked if I could step in for a last-minute hearing, I said yes before he even finished the sentence. Work was my safe place, the one piece of my life that still obeyed rules, logic, evidence. It made sense, unlike everything else.

By noon, I was back from court, heels clicking down the hallway, the faint scent of burnt coffee following me from the break room. I had just sat down, papers fanned across my desk, when a voice came from the doorway.

"Nicole, they need you in the Head Deputy's Office.

I glanced up. The tone was off — too formal, too careful.

When I entered, the air inside felt… wrong. Two supervisors sat around his desk files closed in front of them like props in a scene they didn't want to play. The blinds were half drawn, cutting the light into sharp stripes across the carpet. The green fibers muffled my footsteps.

Something in my chest went tight.

I smiled — that polite, professional smile I'd worn a thousand times. "What's going on?"

No one answered right away. One looked at me, then away. Another shifted, cleared his throat. The silence was unbearable, thick enough to taste.

My palms were slick with sweat. "I started immediately by telling him how much I loved being in VIP. VIP is a special complex litigation unit that handles Sex Crimes and Family Violence cases.

My supervisor told me "Miss Vo..." He pressed his lips together, searching for words. "There's no better way to say this."

My pulse roared in my ears. "What happened?"

He hesitated, then: "You're being arrested."

For a heartbeat, I didn't understand the sentence. It hung in the air like static. Then the floor fell out from under me. This was an attempt by my ex to use legal warfare against me for leaving him.

"The Orange County District Attorney's Office has filed a case against you," he continued, his voice suddenly smaller. "A press release just went out."

A sound filled my head — a high, relentless ringing. My throat burned. I tried to speak, but my tongue felt like it didn't belong to me.

"You're being placed on administrative leave," he cleared his throat, "Effective immediately."

The room blurred at the edges. The fluorescent light above flickered once, twice. I could smell the faint cologne of the investigator standing near the door. I managed to whisper, "I know who's behind this."

He looked away "Pack your things, Nicole." he said quietly. "An investigator will escort you out."

A door opened behind me. The sound of it sliced through the stillness.

Faith in Trials

"Nicole Vo?" The man's voice was flat, official. He didn't wait for confirmation. "You have ten minutes to pack your belongings."

The words hit me like a physical blow. In my head, the words "You're under arrest" kept repeating like a broken record. I'd heard countless times in my career — detached, procedural, part of the job. But hearing them aimed at me was something else entirely. Like someone had swapped lives with me without warning. Thankfully, I was not arrested that day.

They let me gather my things. My daughter's photo. My coffee mug, still faintly warm. Even my placards. Each item felt like an artifact of someone else's life; a woman who'd believed she was safe. When I walked down the hall, heads turned. Conversations stopped mid-sentence. I could feel their eyes, their confusion, their pity. The whispers followed, curling around me like smoke.

"She was always so quiet."

"Do you think it's true?"

"I never would've guessed…"

Each step dragged, thick and slow, like moving through water. And then it hit me—a flash, sharp and cruel. I was seven again, cornered by kids with cruel eyes, their voices a chorus: "Lie, lie!" The sound echoed in my skull. I blinked fast, trying to steady myself, gulping down the tears clawing their way up.

Outside, the sunlight was too bright, almost hostile. The air tasted metallic — fear and shame in equal measure. I wanted to scream. I wanted to run. But I stood still, because that's what people do when they're in shock. They hold themselves perfectly still, hoping reality will skip over them like a wave.

I asked to make a phone call. My hands trembled so hard I nearly dropped the phone. My immediate thought was to call my husband Tim. When he answered, I finally exhaled — the sound ragged, shaky.

"Tim," I said. My voice cracked.

There was a pause, then his steady voice on the other end. "Nicole? What's wrong?"

"I need you to come," I whispered, barely holding it together. "Now."

Chapter Twelve: My God, My Living Hope

A few minutes later, Tim met me outside the building, worry etched across his face. My brother arrived soon after, his own fear hidden behind a shield of determination. We all knew what this was. It was him. The same man who had once vowed that if he couldn't have me, he would destroy me.

My mind was a whirlwind. Every thought collided with another, fear twisting into frustration, despair into panic. I called Kylie's dad, and together we tried to make sense of a world that had suddenly tipped into chaos. We discussed what would happen if I were incarcerated; where Kylie would live, how she would be cared for, and how we could shield her from the storm erupting around us. Everything happened so fast.

Every plan felt both urgent and painfully inadequate. My heart ached with the thought of being separated from her, torn between protecting myself and ensuring her safety. The chaos was overwhelming — sirens, angry voices, flashing lights in my mind — and yet, amid the fear, a sharp clarity lingered: I had to survive, and I had to protect her, no matter the cost. The day was heavy, soaked in disbelief and grief, each second stretching longer than the last.

That afternoon, I met with my friend and defense attorney, HS. I chose him intentionally because of the trust and history we shared. I first met him years earlier when I was serving as a Deputy City Prosecutor, pregnant with Kylie. I had always admired his kindness and integrity; the way he treated everyone in the justice system with sincerity and warmth. He was a man who carried himself with quiet strength and genuine compassion, and those were the qualities I needed most now.

Sitting across from him in his office felt surreal. Just months before, we had laughed together in the courtroom, celebrating verdicts and victories. Now, the roles had reversed in the cruelest way imaginable: I was sitting before him as a client; a defendant, facing scrutiny instead of celebration. The same man whose guidance I had once relied on now studied me with the impartial eyes of the law, and every friendly memory clashed sharply with the cold reality of the present. It was a bitter twist, almost laughable if it weren't so frightening; the irony pressing on me like a weight I couldn't shake. He flipped through the paperwork, shaking his head in disbelief.

"Nicole," he said softly, "this doesn't add up. The evidence is thin. There's no reason this should have been filed."

But it was.

No one — not a single person in my professional circle — could comprehend how this was happening. My reputation in the office had always been one of diligence, ethics, and loyalty. I had built my entire career on pursuing justice. And yet, here I was, facing criminal charges based on lies. The disbelief from colleagues across the board — from the Public Defender's Office to the Private Defense Bar, from Law Enforcement Officers to Judges — spoke volumes. Everyone knew something wasn't right.

I had spent my whole working life as a public servant, giving countless hours in service of justice. But now, I carried a new, bitter title: *Prosecutor Turned Defendant.*

I turned to God angrily. How could this be?

He responded with fierce conviction, *"Nicole, I chose you because I know you are strong enough to handle this."* Those words of discernment stay with me to this day.

There were moments when I continued looked to heaven and asked, *Why would You allow this, God?* And yet, each time I caught myself questioning, I returned to the verse that had become my lifeline:

"For we walk by faith, not by sight." – 2 Corinthians 5:7 (KJV)

Faith in Trials

Faith is when you praise God in the storm, trust Him in the valley, and follow Him in the dark.

Within days, I learned that the Orange County District Attorney's Office had issued a warrant for my arrest labeling me a fugitive despite knowing exactly where I lived, where I worked, and who I was. The insult cut deep, twisting into a mixture of disbelief and fury. My home felt like a cage; every corner seemed to watch me. I didn't leave for days, terrified that any knock at the door could end in handcuffs.

Even simple routines became exercises in anxiety. I was trapped not just by the law, but by the chaos of my own mind; a storm of fear, anger, and helplessness that I couldn't escape. Every moment was a reminder that my life had been upended, and the world outside my door had turned against me in the cruelest, most incomprehensible way.

I felt like a prisoner in my own life.

Occasionally, Tim and I would walk down the street for a meal, but never far. Fear followed us like a shadow.

My mother showed grace beyond words during that time. She brought me food every day, her presence the only warmth in a world that had turned cold. Each meal she prepared carried the silent prayer of a mother's heart. I remember sitting at the table thinking,

How I wish Dad were here.

I missed him more than I could put into words, and I found myself constantly wondering what he would have said, what guidance he would have given me. Would he have told me to fight harder, to stay calm, to protect Kylie no matter what? The absence of his voice made the fear and uncertainty sharper, and I clung to my mother's presence.

Tuesday, April 18, 2017. My arraignment date. Tim and I arrived separately; I rode with my brother. The car was silent—no radio, no conversation, just the hum of tires against asphalt. My stomach churned with a mix of dread and disbelief. Each stoplight felt like a countdown.

When we reached the courthouse, we learned that the assigned Deputy District Attorney hadn't even placed my case on the calendar. HS had to personally request the file from the clerk and have the matter called on record. The disorganization was stunning — almost careless — and it made my chest tighten with frustration and fear. How could something this serious be treated with such disregard?

At one point, Tim noticed the investigator in the hallway. The man refused to look at him, and I felt a flicker of cold anger mixed with anxiety. I wanted answers, a sense of fairness, something to hold onto in the chaos, but there was nothing but silence and avoidance. More than anything, I wanted him to look me in the eye and justify his accusations; to acknowledge the weight of what he was claiming, to confront the reality of the harm he had caused with some shred of accountability.

When my case was finally called, I stood in a courtroom that had once felt like my sanctuary, now transformed into a battlefield. I had spent so much time here before, observing from the gallery, advocating for others, yet now it felt strange, almost disorienting, to see it from this side — the side where I was the one being judged. My brother stood on one side, HS on the other, both trying to mask their anger. I felt a knot of helplessness tighten in my chest, mixed with a spark of resolve: I had to face this, but every step felt like walking through fire. The air was thick with tension, every breath heavy, every heartbeat loud.

The bailiff took my thumbprint after the case was called. The judge ordered that I be booked and released.

So, Tim and I walked to the nearest jail facility to complete the process. I was photographed under harsh fluorescent light — just like every defendant I had ever prosecuted. And in that sterile, humiliating moment, I realized the full weight of what my ex had done.

He hadn't just stolen my peace. He had stolen my identity.

Faith in Trials

As months passed, I sold my home to pay for legal fees. It was a sad moment for me. This was the first home I purchased for Kylie and me. It was our safe place and our home. Tim and I moved into a small apartment that was supposed to be our refuge. But God has a way of testing faith in the places we least expect.

My ex was there too — living one building away.

Out of all the apartment complexes in Orange County, he was my neighbor. There was no escaping him. I'd see him by the mailboxes, the parking lot, even the trash bins. Before stepping outside, I'd scan every corner like a soldier in enemy territory.

Fear became my constant shadow. I felt watched at my own house. I kept the curtains drawn. Fearing, he might be looking in the house. I was losing my sanity.

I began therapy for PTSD. My therapist taught me to say, "I release you," whenever anger surfaced. Forgiveness, she said, didn't mean forgetting. It meant refusing to let the pain define me.

I held on to that truth.

I believe the only reason I survived that season was through forgiveness — choosing peace over bitterness, even when everything in me wanted justice.

"Be thankful in all circumstances, for this is God's will for you." – 1 Thessalonians 5:18 (KJV)

Still, every day felt like walking through fire. I had no income, no health insurance, and the shame of seeing whispers follow me everywhere. Even among colleagues who once respected me, I could feel the unspoken question linger:

What if she really did it?

At night, I prayed by the window, clutching my Bible. "Lord, I don't understand this," I whispered. "Why have You allowed this?"

And yet, even in my tears, a still, quiet voice always answered:

Be still. I am God.

Thankfully, God brought Tim in my life to protect me. He is my angel. With years of being a seasoned Detective, he was determined to search for the truth. I'd watch him from a distance, sifting through thousands of pages of discovery, exhibits, audio recordings, and emails. There were countless nights I witnessed him tossing and turning with unease. The look on his face screamed "there's got to be more." He would not let my freedom be stripped away under his watch. He was determined to crack the case.

My brother never gave up. He hired his own investigators, reviewed every document, searched for truth like a man driven by love and loyalty.

"They're going to see," he told me. "They're going to know this was all lies."

But behind his steady voice, I saw the fear — fear that the same system he trusted might crush the little sister he adored.

Together we organized binders, updated the witness list, reviewed piles of transcripts, and listened to audio recordings over and over again simply because my freedom was on the line.

My mother came to every court date. Her eyes said what her voice couldn't — disbelief that a daughter raised on hard work, faith, and honor could be dragged through such filth.

"We came to America for the dream," she whispered once in the hallway. "Not for this."

And my father — though gone — felt near. I could almost hear his voice echo through my heart: *Case must be dismissed. My daughter's name must be cleared.*

Those words became my anchor. My father was my anchor.

Weeks turned into months. Each hearing brought new delays and indignities. The prosecution withheld discovery, dragged their feet, and treated my life like paperwork. Still, I clung to one of my favorite verses:

Faith in Trials

"Do not be anxious about anything, but instead pray about everything. Tell God what you need and thank Him for all He has done. Then you will experience God's peace, which exceeds anything we can understand." – Philippians 4:6–7 (KJV)

It was during this time, as additional discovery was shared with the Defense, we discovered my ex-husband initiated a complaint with the CA State Bar demanding my license be revoked. The complaint was based on fabricated lies. I found myself once again, hiring another attorney to defend me against his frivolous allegations. The complaint was ultimately deemed "unfounded."

Within 6 months, the Defense was ready for my preliminary hearing. By now we were prepared to move forward anticipating the State's evidence and my Defense.

It was a big day for me. The Court ambiance was all too familiar. I was seated at counsel table next to my brother along with HS and RW. All four of us were not novices, we are seasoned competent trial attorneys. Tim sat in the audience taking copious notes scrutinizing the State's evidence, watching each witness testify.

The preliminary hearing did not scare me because I have conducted hundreds of them throughout my career. My highlighters were meticulously displayed and pens were arranged in the same fashion I normally have when I am conducting *my own preliminary hearing as a prosecutor*. If anyone knew the facts like they were photographic memory, it was me. After all, I was fighting the biggest fight of my life – the Goliath in front of me.

I made a bold and strategic move to testify in my own defense. I had to because I knew the truth. The thought may be scary to a lay person but not to me. I had nothing to hide.

My testimony lasted 2 days. The anxiety rushed through my body as I walked up to the witness stand and took the oath to tell the truth. As I sat at the witness stand, I was confused. The level of State's organization demonstrated lack of preparation and knowledge of the case. And so on direct examination, I carefully listened to every question and answered with conviction speaking what I knew to be true.

I didn't ask for any breaks; I do recall asking for questions to be rephrased when they sounded confusing. When I answered the last question at the witness stand, I did not feel defeated. I felt confident God had carried me through the waters.

At the end of the hearing, the Judge even had concerns why the case was filed. After all the evidence was presented, it was clear the criminal case was guised under the veil of a bitter divorce.

Then one night, my brother called. His voice trembled — not with fear, but with hope. He had found an email thread buried in discovery: proof that my ex had threatened to expose the DA's office in the media unless they filed charges against me.

It was extortion — and it was the truth we needed.

I fell to my knees. For the first time in months, I wept with gratitude instead of despair. My body shook, not from fear, but from relief, from the overwhelming weight of knowing I was not alone. The tension I had carried for weeks — the constant anxiety, the gnawing uncertainty, the suffocating fear — began to unravel in a flood of tears.

"Thank You, Lord," I whispered, my eyes closed as tears rolled down my cheeks. "You said You would fight for me. I see it now." In that moment, every sleepless night, every moment of dread, every tear shed in silence, felt acknowledged, transformed into a strange kind of strength. I felt a lightness in my chest, a quiet assurance that, even in the darkest storm, I was being carried by God.

The truth began to unravel. So did my ex's control. His lies collapsed under their own weight. While my case was pending my ex was eventually arrested and charged himself by the same office that once charged me, I felt no joy; only release.

On my drive to the courthouse, for another pre-trial hearing, the Holy Spirit whispered to me: *Nicole, you will demand your trial today.*

Faith in Trials

I've had moments of discernment before, fleeting nudges in my heart, but this one was different; sharp, urgent, unshakable. It pierced through the fog of fear and doubt, leaving no room for hesitation. My future, everything I had fought for, depended on this single act of courage.

As I stepped into the courtroom that morning. I felt every eye on me, every judgment hanging heavy, and yet the voice inside me burned brighter than any fear. I drew a steadying breath and spoke the words aloud, each syllable a declaration of defiance and faith:

"Your Honor, I am demanding my trial."

The room seemed to hold its breath, suspended in that moment of audacity — a moment where fear met resolve, and everything hung in the balance. I could feel all eyes on me. But it didn't matter; I knew God was watching it. That was all I needed.

And one year after my nightmare began, the court dismissed my case.

No grand explanation. No apology. Just a single line in the record that changed everything: *Case dismissed.*

I walked out of that courthouse into the California sunlight and finally exhaled. The warmth of the day kissed my face, and for the first time in months, I felt air fill my lungs without the weight of dread pressing down. I wasn't the same woman who had walked into that storm. I was stripped bare, refined by fire, and quietly rebuilt. Each step on the sun-warmed pavement felt like reclamation, a declaration that I had survived and would not be broken.

That evening, I returned to the same church pond where I had once written in my journal, begging God for clarity. The water lay perfectly still, reflecting the sky brushed in gold and amber, the last light of day spilling across the surface like a promise. A gentle breeze whispered through the trees, and in the hush, I felt a presence — a still, undeniable certainty. And then I heard His voice again:

Be still and know that I am God.*-Psalms 46:10 (KJV)*

Nicole Vo

For years, I had been in courtrooms, standing for cases that always began with *The People versus…*, never imagining that one day, the words of authority and judgment would feel directed at me; not as someone judging, but as someone judged. It wasn't irony; it was reality hitting me hard.

When the system had failed me, when it seemed like every door was closed, I realized that I hadn't been abandoned. That was the real victory. Sitting by the pond, watching the sun sink lower in the sky, I felt a sense of relief and clarity I hadn't known in months. This wasn't about a courtroom win or a verdict — it was about knowing that, somehow, I had been seen, protected, and brought through the worst of it.

Chapter Thirteen: Rebuilding

There is a quiet that follows a storm; not silence exactly, but a softness. A gentleness that wraps itself around the debris, whispering, '*You survived.*'

After my case was dismissed, after the headlines stopped, after the courtroom lights dimmed, I found myself standing in the stillness, looking at the pieces of a life that had been shaken apart. The year before had stripped me of dignity, peace, and certainty. But it had not stripped me of God. And that made all the difference.

When I was placed on administrative leave, it felt like exile. I wasn't allowed to speak to anyone in the office; not colleagues, not friends, not even the people who had once celebrated my victories with me. One day I was in the courtroom fighting for children; the next, I was sitting at home in silence, wondering if the career I had built with sweat and sacrifice was slipping through my fingers.

Walking back into the office after the dismissal felt like stepping into a room where time had paused, but curiosity hadn't. Conversations quieted when I passed. Eyes lingered. People wondered:

Why was she prosecuted?

What evidence did they have?

How did it all get dismissed?

And yet, beneath the curiosity, something else pulsed: relief. Genuine, heartfelt relief.

My coworkers—people who had seen me fight for victims, who had watched me pour myself into cases—knew in their hearts that I had been wrongfully accused. Their hugs were tight, their smiles unrestrained. One colleague whispered, "We prayed for you. We knew your character. We knew this wasn't who you were."

For the first time, as I write this book, I am sharing pieces of my story; how it felt to be both prosecutor and defendant, how faith became my anchor, how God held me when the world felt hostile. I wasn't just returning to work. I was returning to a community that had quietly held space for me.

But the emotional damage was real. What I had endured with my ex-husband, the trauma of betrayal, the loneliness of standing accused, those wounds didn't disappear overnight. Still, there was something inside me stronger than grief. A voice that whispered,

'Keep going. You have a story to tell.'

I had no idea back then that the story would become this book. That the pain I carried would one day be stitched into chapters that might heal someone else. I didn't know God was shaping my testimony. I only knew He was sustaining me.

Looking back now, I realize: I am the narrator, but God is the true author. Every tear, every trial, every victory; He wrote them with purpose.

The financial cost of the year nearly broke me, too. Legal fees. Lost income. Bills piling up like accusations. But even here, God was weaving provision into every gap. Family stepped in. Friends surrounded me. Doors opened that should have stayed shut. Somehow, what should have ruined me simply didn't.

People often say, "God can restore what was lost." What they don't tell you is that sometimes He restores it tenfold.

I'd like to invite you to read the story of "Job" in the Bible. Job was a God-fearing man blessed in so many ways by the Lord. Then one day, his world shattered. Everything God had given to him was taken away. God even made him suffer from a serious health condition. I'd like to believe that my story parallels Job's story. Everything I had was taken away by the Lord. But despite our sufferings, we both praised God during the storms, and through our unwavering faith, the Lord blessed us tenfold.

Faith in Trials

When the storm lifted, I could feel the shift. The air felt lighter. My body exhaled. My spirit stood taller. Tim and I sat at the kitchen table one night, both of us tired but hopeful, and we said, almost in unison, "It's time for a fresh start."

We found our forever home not long after; a place filled with light, warmth, and the kind of peace you feel in your bones. I remember standing in the living room, sunlight pouring through the windows, thinking,

This is what redemption looks like.

We painted walls. We unpacked boxes. We prayed in each room. And with every step, I felt God whispering, *I promised you a brighter future. Here it is.*

The battle was over. I fought the good fight and we won.

Shortly after settling into our new home, I received the assignment that felt like a divine exhale: I was placed back into the same Complex Litigation Unit I had been in before the charges.

Back to the cases I loved. Back to the children whose stories shaped my calling. Back to the purpose God had placed inside me long before I understood it.

Some people think purpose is a straight line. Mine had looped through storms, valleys, trials, and miracles but it brought me back to where I belonged.

Protecting children. Giving them a voice. Standing in the gap.

It felt like coming full circle. Because even though I once dreamed of being a teacher, God placed me in a different kind of classroom, one where the lessons were written in courage, justice, and compassion.

I used to believe my childhood dream of teaching had died when I was forced into law. But now I see clearly. I did become a teacher, just not in the way I expected. I teach jurors the law and how to apply the facts of the to the law. I teach victims about hope. I teach the world that justice is worth fighting for.

My life came in full circle in ways I never could have imagined.

And just when everything felt peaceful again—when the sun was shining, when the air finally felt safe—a new warning whispered through my body. A sign I tried to ignore.

It started with a headache. Then pressure behind my eyes. Then a migraine so sharp it felt like lightning exploding inside my skull. I grabbed the counter to steady myself, a chill racing through me.

The storm was over. But something new was beginning. The body, after all, always speaks. And this time…it wasn't whispering.

It was screaming.

Chapter Fourteen: A Friend in Him

Stress does not arrive all at once.

It accumulates.

It gathers quietly, stacking itself on the body in places you do not see at first. It hides behind words like commitment, duty, calling. It convinces you that exhaustion is just the price of purpose, that weariness is evidence of faithfulness.

When I returned to the same unit I had once been assigned to, it felt like coming home. These were the cases I loved. Not because they were easy — they never were — but because they mattered. Protecting children was never just a function of my job. It was a responsibility I carried with reverence.

Every case file represented a child who had already lost everything. Every courtroom appearance felt like standing between innocence and irreversible harm. I believed, without question, that this was exactly where God had placed me. I did not feel heroic. I felt useful.

There is a privilege in being trusted with other people's pain, a privilege carried carefully. I knew the emotional cost of this work, but I believed the cost was worth paying if it meant one more child slept safely at night.

They say prosecutors should only stay in my unit for about five years. After that, the work begins to take a toll — mentally, emotionally, physically. The images stay. The testimony replays itself when the house is quiet. The stories embed themselves in your nervous system and resurface when you least expect them.

I stayed fourteen years.

At the time, it never felt excessive. It did not feel dangerous. It did not feel like sacrifice. It felt like stewardship. Like obedience. Like

God entrusted me with something sacred, and walking away would mean abandoning children who still needed protection.

By then, I was one of the most senior attorneys in the unit. I was known as a "trial machine." On average, I handled seven to eight complex trials every year. These were not routine cases. They involved multiple child victims and defendants facing life in prison. Every decision mattered. Every word mattered. There was no room for fatigue, no margin for error.

And I delivered.

I prepared relentlessly. I lived inside my files. I memorized testimony. I anticipated defenses. I stood firm in court, composed and controlled, even when the evidence was unbearable. Judges trusted me. Jurors listened. Children felt safe with me.

What I did not realize was that my body was keeping a separate record.

Then the office changed.

There was a mass exodus — attorneys leaving for other units, other offices, other lives. Files piled higher. Calendars tightened. We became understaffed almost overnight.

Several prosecutors left my special unit. Their cases did not disappear. They landed on my desk.

As the most senior attorney, I absorbed the burden. I took on their trials, their deadlines, and their emotional labor. I did not protest or hesitate. I told myself I could handle it. I always had.

One of the last trials I completed during that period was not even mine. I inherited it because we were short-staffed. It involved five child victims. A life sentence case for the perpetrator.

I had one month to prepare.

One month.

Normally, a child sexual assault case involving even one or two victims takes a year — sometimes longer — before it is ready for a jury. Evidence must be meticulously reviewed. Experts consulted. Children prepared so they are not retraumatized by the process. Each detail must be airtight.

But that was not my reality.

The pressure was immediate and suffocating. One month to prepare a case of that magnitude was unheard of. I could feel the stress settle into my chest, my jaw, my temples. Sleep became fragmented, meals were skipped without thought, exercise disappeared entirely.

This case felt different. I could tell.

Still, I powered through. I fought hard. I fought relentlessly. I had to. I stood in court day after day, determined to vindicate the rights of those children. I refused to let the lack of time compromise justice.

The cost was immeasurable, but we finished the trial.

I did not yet recognize that my body was warning me.

I began falling.

Not metaphorically — physically.

At first, it was subtle. A stumble here. A moment of dizziness there. I brushed it off. I blamed fatigue. Stress. Long hours. Then it became more frequent. I would lose my balance without warning. My thoughts sometimes lagged behind my words.

Sleep deprivation became my worst enemy.

Still, I pushed forward.

After finishing that trial, I immediately began another child sexual abuse case — another life case. There was no pause. No recovery. Just momentum.

The day everything changed, we were already in court. Jury selection was about to begin.

I knew something was wrong.

I requested a chambers conference with the judge and counsel. My voice was calm, professional, controlled — the same voice I had used for years.

"I just want to advise the court," I said, "that I've been experiencing falls. If it happens during trial, please don't be alarmed."

The Judge studied me carefully, his concern was evident.

I reassured him. I always did.

That evening, I brought my laptop home and continued preparing for trial. I reviewed exhibits. Drafted outlines. Refined questions. My husband watched me uneasily from across the room.

I did not see it yet, but my body did. ENOUGH!

My head fell forward — hard — onto the laptop. The sound echoed through the room like something breaking. My husband rushed to me, calling my name. I was not responding the way I should have been.

Fear took over his voice.

He turned to my daughter.

"Call 911."

The sirens blurred into the night as the ambulance rushed me to the hospital. I remember fragments — flashing lights against dark windows, the sterile smell of antiseptic, voices moving too fast for my mind to follow. My husband's face hovered above me, tight with fear, his voice calling my name again and again as if anchoring me to the world.

In the emergency room, everything became urgent. Nurses moved quickly, cutting away the calm I had carried for years. I was placed on a gurney, wires attached, questions fired at me faster than I could answer. Somewhere in the chaos, I felt the unmistakable sense that something was deeply wrong — not the kind of wrong that passes with rest, but the kind that demands surrender.

They rushed me into a CT scan.

Minutes later, the room felt heavier. The doctor returned, his expression grave. He explained that there was a brain bleed in the front left portion of my brain — the area responsible for executive functioning. Decision-making. Reasoning. Control.

The irony was cruel. The very part of my brain that had allowed me to function under pressure, to lead trials, to manage chaos — was now failing.

Then came the words that stopped time.

"You need emergency brain surgery."

I laughed — not because it was funny, but because it was impossible.

"That's not possible," I said. "I'm in the middle of trial. Can't we re-schedule this in 2 weeks?"

The neurosurgeon looked at me, stunned. Then his voice rose, sharp and unyielding.

"Did you not HEAR me?" he shouted. "You will die if you don't have this surgery!"

In that moment, the illusion of control shattered. There was no negotiation, no compromise, no courtroom argument. My life had narrowed to one choice: surrender or die.

Needless to say, we know who won that argument.

They prepared me for surgery quickly. Consent forms. IVs. Bright lights overhead. I remember being wheeled down a hallway, the ceiling tiles passing one by one above me. I tried to pray, but the words felt distant, scattered. All I could manage was a whisper.

"God… please."

Then everything went dark.

They performed a craniotomy — opening my skull to stop the bleeding and save my life. When I woke up, twenty-two staples held my head together. The pain was immediate and overwhelming, like a deep ache that pulsed with every heartbeat.

I was in the ICU.

It was a miracle I woke up at all.

God is so good.

At first, I didn't understand what had happened. My brain hurt in a way I had never experienced before. Morphine dulled the pain but also blurred reality. Time became meaningless. Days passed without memory. I drifted in and out of consciousness, surrounded by beeping machines and hushed voices.

I spent six days in the ICU, heavily medicated. Even after I was discharged home, large portions of that time remain missing from my memory. Conversations happened that I do not remember. Decisions were made without my awareness. Life moved forward while I was suspended somewhere between awake and gone.

When I finally became more lucid, reality still hadn't landed.

I truly believed I would be back at work in two weeks.

That belief carried me for a while — until my body made it clear that the woman I had been no longer existed in the way I remembered her.

Then depression arrived at my doorstep.

It didn't announce itself with tears at first. It settled in slowly. I was bedridden. Weak. Dizzy. Disoriented. Simple tasks felt monumental. Walking across a room required effort I didn't have. My thoughts felt slower, less sharp. Words escaped me mid-sentence.

I didn't recognize myself.

I grieved the old Nicole.

The one who never stopped.

The one who thrived under pressure.

The one who believed endurance was strength.

Faith in Trials

I mourned her like a death — because in many ways, she was gone.

There was no courtroom to return to. No trials to prepare for. No identity to hide behind. Without my work, I felt exposed, stripped down to something raw and unfamiliar.

Every day became about small victories.

Sitting up in bed without dizziness.

Taking a few steps without falling.

Remembering a word that had slipped away moments earlier.

Each accomplishment felt insignificant compared to the life I had lived before — and yet, they were everything now.

I had to relearn patience with my body, my mind, and myself.

And in that stillness, something unexpected happened.

God became close.

Not the God of victories and courtroom wins.

Not the God I invoked before trials.

But the God who sat with me in silence when I had nothing left to offer.

He did not demand productivity. He did not measure my worth by outcomes. He did not ask me to be strong.

He simply stayed.

For the first time, my faith was not something I used. It was something I leaned on. God became less of a protector in front of me — and more of a companion beside me. My friend.

I began to understand that my body had not betrayed me — it had saved me. Every fall, every warning sign, every moment of collapse was my body pleading for mercy I refused to give myself.

Looking back, I see it clearly now: I did not stop because I was weak. I stopped because I had reached the limit of what one human being can carry.

The work had been sacred. But so was rest.

The children I fought for mattered deeply. But so did the woman who fought for them.

Rebuilding did not happen all at once. It happened slowly, unevenly, day by day. Some days I felt hopeful. Others, defeated. Some days I longed desperately for my old life. Others, I felt grateful to simply be alive.

I learned to celebrate progress instead of perfection.

I learned that healing is not linear.

And I learned that faith is not proven in how much you can endure — but in how willing you are to trust when everything familiar has been taken away.

I wasn't being punished, I was being preserved.

God did not remove me from the courtroom to diminish me. He removed me to save my life. To teach me that identity rooted solely in service will eventually collapse — but identity rooted in Him will hold, even when everything else falls apart.

In the quiet of recovery, stripped of titles and momentum, I learned something I had never allowed myself to believe before:

I was still worthy — even when I could do nothing.

And in that realization, I found Him not as a judge, not as a commander, but as a friend who never left my side.

Chapter Fifteen: God Is Still Writing My Story

There was a time when looking back felt dangerous.

The memories were sharp, the emotions still close enough to touch. Pain had a way of pulling me under, of convincing me that what happened defined who I was. Fear lived in the past tense, yet it echoed loudly enough to feel present.

Now, when I look back, it feels different.

Not because the pain was not real. It was.

Not because the fear did not shape me. It did.

Not because the uncertainty did not leave its mark. It mattered more than I knew at the time.

It feels different because I am no longer standing where I once stood.

I can acknowledge what happened without reliving it. I can honor the weight of those seasons without carrying them on my shoulders every day. The wounds are part of my story, but they are no longer the narrator.

There is gratitude here now. Not for the suffering itself, but for the growth it produced. For the strength I did not know I had. For the faith that survived even when I was not sure I would.

I am not the same person who began this journey.

Growth does not erase the past. It reframes it. It allows me to say, this was hard. This hurt. And I am still here.

Fear still whispers. It still asks questions. It still tries to predict outcomes and protect against pain. The difference now is that fear no longer leads. It no longer decides. It no longer gets the final word.

I did not come out of these chapters with answers neatly tied together.

What I carry instead are lessons. Quiet ones. Earned ones. Valuable ones.

Trusting God in silence may have been the hardest lesson of all. There were seasons when prayers felt unanswered and direction felt withheld. No signs. No clarity. Just stillness. I used to believe silence meant absence. It does not. It meant the answers to my prayers were delayed.

Surrender became a daily choice, not a single moment. Some days it was graceful. Other days it was reluctant. Still, it mattered. Each time I chose surrender, even imperfectly, I loosened fear's grip and strengthened trust.

And rest came last.

Not because it was unimportant, but because I did not know how to allow it. Rest required faith in timing. It required believing that pausing did not mean failing and waiting did not mean being forgotten. It meant God was working *all things for good* even though I could not see it.

These lessons are not rules to follow. They are tools I now carry. I use them when fear resurfaces, when control tempts me again, when silence stretches longer than I would like.

I am stronger, not because I avoided hardship, but because I remained standing through it. I am resilient, not because I never broke, but because I learned how to rebuild. God never left my side.

The focus has shifted.

There was a time when I believed I needed answers before I could move forward.

I waited for clarity. For certainty. For the reassurance that I would not make another wrong step. But life rarely offers that kind of resolution. Faith was never meant to be built on having everything explained.

Faith in Trials

It was meant to be built on trust.

Life may still feel uncertain at times. Questions may remain unanswered. But solitude is no longer part of the journey. I am not moving forward alone, and neither are you.

Faith does not promise ease. It promises companionship.

And that is enough to keep going.

Chapter Sixteen: Embracing the New Nicole

After a traumatic brain injury, I learned the battle is not just physical.

There are two battles you face. One is the injury itself. The other is learning how to live in a world that does not fully understand what you are carrying. People may see the outward progress, but they do not see the daily effort it takes just to function. They do not feel the exhaustion, the frustration, or the grief that comes with losing abilities I once took for granted.

During my most difficult moments, pain was constant and discouragement came easily. There were days when everything felt overwhelming and strength felt out of reach. In those moments, I had a choice. I could focus on how broken I felt, or I could place what I could not carry into God's hands.

I chose to entrust my faith to Him.

There was a moment when I heard clearly from the Lord. He spoke my name and said that He had taken me out for a reason. He told me He intervened because He knew I was going to die. Those words stayed with me. They were not spoken in fear, but in purpose. In that moment, I understood that my life had been spared intentionally. I am still here because God was not finished with me.

Healing did not come quickly. It did not come on my timeline. Healing unfolded slowly, according to the Lord's timing. I learned God and I do not use the same watch. For nearly two and a half years, God watched me grow through pain, grief, and despair. He saw how difficult even the simplest tasks became. Thinking, bathing, brushing my teeth, washing my hair, getting dressed, standing alone, walking alone, cooking, reading, writing, and driving were no longer things I could do without effort. The abilities I once moved through without thought were taken from me.

Faith in Trials

Through that loss, I learned humility.

I battled fear and frustration when my doctors doubted, I would ever practice law again. Their prognosis tried to define my future, but it was a destiny I refused to accept.

I was determined to heal and return to a sense of normalcy. Learning how to write again required me to purchase Kindergarten level books to learn how to hold a pen and write within the lines. To practice reading, I learned it must be done in baby steps. One sentence at a time. Then a paragraph. Then a whole page. These small victories meant the world to me.

There were so many moments when I could not see the solution. I could not see the outcome. I could not see how things would ever improve. The hope of one day returning to work felt distant and out of reach. Yet while I was waiting, God was working for my good. What felt like stillness was not absence. It was preparation.

The hard times crushed my spirit, but God promised to carry me through every storm and every deep water. He promised to never let me go. And He has kept that promise.

Chapter Seventeen: What God Has Taught My Heart

Before my injury, my life was built on independence.

I was a single mother. I worked hard. I stayed busy. I believed that being strong meant being in control and being capable at all times. My career and my responsibilities defined my sense of purpose. I rarely slowed down, and I rarely questioned that pace. I thought I was carrying everything on my own.

What I did not fully recognize then was who had been carrying me.

In my brokenness, I discovered how close God truly is to the brokenhearted. When my spirit felt crushed and my confidence weakened, His presence did not pull away. It drew nearer. I was not abandoned in my pain. I was held in it.

The journey through healing changed the way I see life. Trauma gave me a new lens. I no longer measure success by productivity or output. I learned to slow down, even when every instinct told me to push harder. I learned that rest is not a reward for exhaustion. It is a necessity for healing.

God taught me how to care for myself without guilt. He showed me the importance of setting boundaries and honoring limits. I learned that grace is not something I only extend to others. It is something I am allowed to give myself. Forgiveness included forgiving myself for what I could not do and for the time it took to recover.

Work no longer defines my worth. Achievement no longer determines my value. My identity is not rooted in how much I produce, how much I accomplish, or how much I can handle. It is rooted in who I am and whose I am.

Faith in Trials

I learned that I am allowed to restart. I am allowed to refocus. I am allowed to reset as many times as I need to, without shame or explanation.

Choosing myself became part of choosing healing. Loving myself was not selfish. It was necessary. I began to pursue becoming healthier, more present, more whole. Not to return to who I was, but to step into who I am becoming.

Pain no longer feels permanent. I have learned that what I am experiencing now is not the end of the story. Joy has been promised, and I believe it is coming. This season has given me a second chance at life, and I do not take that lightly.

Everything I lost refined me. Everything I endured taught me. And everything God restored reminded me that purpose often comes through what we never would have chosen.

Scripture has come alive in my life. When God says He will restore health and heal wounds, I believe Him. When Jesus reminds us that what is impossible with man is possible with God, I stand as evidence of that truth. God has kept His promises, and He continues to do so.

This journey has shown me that where I am today is not where I will remain. My present situation is not my final destination. Everything God does has a purpose, even when it unfolds in ways we do not understand.

The best is still ahead.

Final Thoughts From the Author

You may ask why I chose to write this book?

The pain I endured is not to be wasted. From overcoming two failed marriages, juggling a demanding career as a single parent, grieving the loss of a parent, surviving domestic violence, fighting wrongful criminal prosecution, and healing after a traumatic brain injury, I learned His plan was to use my pain to help others who are suffering. There is hope.

Looking back, the pain was heartbreaking, but I understand why he chose me to endure it. My pain produced character and character produced perseverance. It has made me who I am today.

Right now, you may be suffering. You may feel damaged, discouraged, depressed, debilitated, defeated, delayed, denied, deserted, and disappointed.

You may ask, **"What do I do when my plans do not match God's plan?"** This is what I did and I hope some or all the suggestions can help you. Surrender- When you surrender, truly surrender- and release your grip on control, you begin to experience the peace of God.

Even when the waves crashed violently and the end of the storm was nowhere in sight-at least that's how it felt at the time-I kept moving. And then, I finally gave it all to God.

Financially, I became destitute. I lost my job and the health insurance that came with it. I fought relentlessly to preserve my bar license. I stood eye to eye against the Goliath in front of me-defending myself against wrongful charges. And with every ounce of strength I had left, I was determined to heal from brain surgery.

In the end, I understood something extremely profound: the only pathway to peace was complete surrender. Not partial. Not conditional. Everything. I placed my fears in the hands of the "Big Man" upstairs and I always kept my eyes on Him.

Faith in Trials

Choose faith over fear – When you don't understand, don't worry; pray about it. Worry does not solve our problems. The phrase "Do not be afraid" is repeated 365 times in the bible. One for each day of the year. God did not give us a spirit of fear, but he gave us a spirit of faith. In a time of chaos continue to chose faith over fear.

1. Pray without ceasing – Pray until your situation changes. Remember there is never a "bad" time to pray. God is here for you all the time. Pray, no matter what time of day. God doesn't tell you return because he's sick, on break, on vacation, or resting at the moment. Heaven's door does not have a sign that says, "Will be right back." God wants you to draw near to him so that you can call him "my friend," and I always kept my eyes on him.

2. God says to me and to you, "Rest. I am already at work. I will turn around every negative situation in your life and will bless you. I will heal every place you are hurting."

3. When I was slapped with a frivolous civil lawsuit seeking $2 million in damages, I refused give up. I kept fighting.

4. When thoughts raced through my mind that I could face incarceration for a very long time, I was reminded to "Be still and know that He is God."

5. The anxiety of losing my bar license was crushing because being a trial attorney defined my purpose and identity. I prayed the Lord would protect me against these false allegations so that I wouldn't lose my job or the prospect of practicing law ever again in any capacity.

6. When I faced depression from being temporarily disabled, I prayed daily for things to change. I wanted to work and feel I had purpose in life. Then one day, I had a moment of discernment. God told me to "Look up and get up." I did exactly what he commanded me to do. Within minutes I made calls to my Dr. and my HR department asking to "Return to Work". That same day, within hours, I received

an email to report to work the following day! God is so good.

7. Trust that God is in control – Believe it even when things look out of control. He knows exactly what he is doing. We don't see what he sees, nor do we know what he knows. That is why is he God and we are not.

8. Be patient. God does not make mistakes. God is still writing your story. He knows what he's doing. God's timing is never early, never late, but always on time.

9. Look for the good – He can bring good out of the bad things in our lives. Our hardships can help us learn so much from our fears and failures. In every painful situation, look for the hidden treasures yet to be discovered.

10. Be thankful in all circumstances- Be grateful for his blessings, his provisions, his mercy, and his grace.

Pain in life is inevitable. In these trying times, I didn't accept defeat. I trusted him. He already knew it was not the end of my story but a chapter in my life. And I trust the *next* chapter because I know the author.

Miracles happen every day, so don't stop believing in God's grace.

I want to leave you with this -Remember God's strength is made perfect in your weakness. That's where he shows up in our lives. With faith and hope, all things are possible.

www.ingramcontent.com/pod-product-compliance
Ingram Content Group UK Ltd.
Pitfield, Milton Keynes, MK11 3LW, UK
UKHW060117010826
14089UKWH00004B/39

9 798993 283159